MORE PRAISE FOR *STANDING AT WATER'S EDGE*

"The perfect book if you're experiencing a dry spell in your creativity — a step-by-step path to inspiration."

— Armando Gallo, photographer and member of the
Hollywood Foreign Press Association board of directors

"This book combines insights gained from contemporary psychoanalytic theory and practical, "hands-on" recommendations for encouraging creativity. Reading this book will reward not only artists but also all those who desire to express themselves in new ways but do not know how or where to begin. As a psychoanalyst deeply involved in the study of creativity, I consider this book as serving an important function in tapping a variety of creative resources."

— Anna Ornstein, MD, professor emerita in child psychiatry
at the University of Cincinnati and
lecturer in psychiatry at Harvard Medical School

"Dr. Paris's book could not have arrived at a better moment: I was cut off from my creativity, sad over lost love, and afraid I'd never feel that rush of immersion again. Her stories and suggestions helped me move forward, but here's why you must buy this book: Dr. Paris brilliantly explores how our fears and blocks prevent us from entering the creative immersion we all crave."

— Jennifer Louden, author of *The Woman's Comfort Book*
and *The Life Organizer*

Standing at Water's Edge

Moving Past Fear, Blocks,
and Pitfalls to Discover the
Power of Creative Immersion

Anne Paris, PhD

New World Library
Novato, California

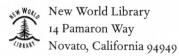

New World Library
14 Pamaron Way
Novato, California 94949

Text design by Tona Pearce Myers

Library of Congress Cataloging-in-Publication Data
Paris, Anne, 1962–
Standing at water's edge : moving past fears, blocks, and pitfalls to discover the power of creative immersion / Anne Paris.
    p.   cm.
Includes bibliographical references and index.
ISBN 978-1-57731-589-6 (pbk. : alk. paper)
    1. Creative ability—Psychological aspects. 2. Inspiration. 3. Creation (Literary, artistic, etc.) I. Title.
BF410.P37 2008
153.3'5—dc22   2008003402

First printing, May 2008
ISBN: 978-1-57731-589-6

Printed in the United States on 50% postconsumer-waste recycled paper

g New World Library is a proud member of the Green Press Initiative.

10 9 8 7 6 5 4 3 2 1

FOR MIKE

Contents

Introduction

How do we take the plunge into creativity? If you are an artist, a writer, or a person who works in any other creative capacity, this book is for you. It draws on my twenty years of experience as a clinical psychologist in understanding and helping all types of artists along in their creative processes. Through thousands of hours of psychotherapy sessions with artists, I have learned to respect artistic creation as one of the most challenging of all human activities. As I accompanied these artists, writers, actors, dancers, designers, and musicians on their artistic journeys, I witnessed their inner struggles as they wrestled with beginning and sustaining the creative process. I have seen artists who had become depressed or had developed addictions. The process of creativity was obviously an intense psychological challenge, one that promised ultimate gratification but also carried the risk of pain and darkness.

Creating a piece of art is one form of immersive experience. But so are our relationships with others. For example, allowing myself to trust someone else, being able to enter into my son's view of the world, and being able to play with my friends all call for a capacity to both invest myself and suspend myself. These immersive moments are what define "me" and give meaning and strength to my existence. And yet the anticipation of immersing myself is, at times, very frightening and calls up my strongest psychological defenses.

Adding insights from my own struggles to immerse to those I

have observed in artist clients, I hope to present a framework of understanding that will help others. As a psychologist, I have understood that many problems arise from the inability to fully immerse oneself, whether that is in the formation of something new (like art or scholarly work) or in the creation of a loving and intimate connection with another person. Through my personal and professional experiences, I began to appreciate the process of creativity involved in everyday life and to see similarities in the blocks encountered. My theoretical framework is based in contemporary psychoanalytic ideas and research. Rather than aiming to offer quick fixes for blocks to immersion, my goal is to provide the reader with a deep appreciation and respect for immersive efforts. This book will be about the depth of the fears that paralyze us and about how to elicit the kinds of psychological support we need to boost our courage and capacity to take the plunge into creativity and hope.

Although my main focus is on the experience of artistic creation, the ideas presented here extend to all kinds of creative activity. Therefore, if you are seeking to increase your creativity in business, academics, or other areas, this book can help you as well.

By focusing on the internal experience of artists as they enter into and sustain creativity, I will reveal the hidden but powerful influence of their sense of connection with others on their creative capacities. This book explores how the capacity to immerse into creativity is a deeply rooted psychological journey that engages our most fundamental hopes and fears. You will likely find yourself in these pages, and I hope that you emerge feeling more special, safe, and understood. Through this appreciation, you will gain new self-awareness that will propel you beyond artistic blocks you encounter along the way. Artists need to understand how creativity confronts them with their deepest fears; how blocks and fears can lead to psychological problems such as depression and addiction, and how to avoid these pitfalls; and how relationships with others are crucial in the creative process. This book will describe what kinds of relationships support creativity, how childhood experience plays an important role in the creative process, and how one can psychologically navigate the creative process from the start to the finish of an artistic project.

I will focus on the part of the creative process that is often the most difficult: entering into a creative state. The capacity to dive into creativity, both in beginning a project and in having to begin again every day as the project continues, will determine our productivity as well as our sense of fulfillment and gratification. Whether you are a professional artist or a hobby artist, you have probably encountered blocks in your process. See if you can relate to the feelings Mary expresses in the following example. Mary squirmed in her chair as she explained,

> I just don't know what is wrong with me. Why can't I just do it? I feel stressed all the time when I'm not writing. 'I should be writing,' I say to myself, but I don't. I think, if I just get the laundry done, then I'll be free to sit down and write the next chapter. But then I don't. Maybe I need to exercise first, and I go for a run. I get back home, fully intending to sit down at the computer. But I don't. And all the while I'm feeling bad and stressed about not writing. What is wrong with me? Maybe I'm just lazy. Or maybe unconsciously I don't really want to write. Or maybe it just means that I'm not really cut out to be a writer. 'Writers write,' I tell myself.
>
> Then I just spiral downward. I feel so bad, so completely *unable* to sit down and write. I've read all the books. 'Set aside a time for writing each day.' I do that . . . some days I'm actually able to write something, and it feels so good. So why don't I do it the next day?
>
> Anyway, I'm in another depression about it right now. It seems like the more I pressure myself to write, the less I'm able to do it. I begin to doubt my book idea. Sometimes I am convinced that it has absolutely no value, has been done before, and that I have no business thinking that I can write. Then I

even begin to doubt my entire self. Maybe I'm just a big fraud. The other things I've had published were just flukes. I can really get depressed sometimes. I even start to withdraw from my husband and kids. Why do I do this to myself?

But then the times that I get on a roll — sometimes I can hammer out ten to fifteen pages at a time, without a break, without a breath. That feels so wonderful, like this is exactly who I am, and everything I've ever experienced has led me to this place.

How am I able to do it sometimes? I have no idea. If I knew that, I wouldn't be here, sitting in your office. What should I do? What's the trick that I'm not getting? Or maybe I should stop torturing myself and just give up on writing. Why is it so damned hard?

Mary is certainly not alone in her struggle to create. In fact, most artists I have worked with share the experience of being both drawn to and repelled from the creative process. Countless books have been written about the process of creation, and most of them acknowledge the artist's internal struggle to start. However, most of the literature I have seen offers behavioral remedies for this problem: "Set aside a time and place every day for the creative endeavor" or "You must exercise a great deal of self-discipline." I agree that structure can certainly help an artist to focus and discipline his time. But most artists do not find the strength to overcome deeply embedded blocks with this advice. "If it was that easy, I'd do it," they say.

I recognized the need for a book for artists that would address these deeper psychological experiences. I want to put into words what artists feel as they move through the creative process so they can feel understood and less alone. By engaging with artists' inner worlds, I have understood psychological needs that often go unnoticed or are misunderstood. I have come to understand that the moment of entry into the creative state actually relies upon the artist's most deeply embedded assumptions about his or her psychological survival and safety. The difficulty and risk to the artist's core self in this moment deserve to be appreciated, understood, and respected.

In my clinical practice, I specialize in parenting and relationships as well as in creativity. I will apply my understandings in these other areas to the creative process: this book will show how the nature of the artist's childhood experiences and the nature of her relationships with others shape her creative process. I believe it is critical that the artist feel understood, at any point in time, in the context of both her inner and her outer world. This book reveals a more complete understanding of the person engaged in the creative process and the psychological hurdles she faces along the way. With this increased appreciation, many artists have been able to emerge from creative blocks and move on to completion of their projects.

The development of these ideas about creativity began when I decided to facilitate a psychotherapy support group for adult survivors of sexual abuse. At the time, I specialized in treating victims of trauma such as abuse, incest, and rape. I ran an ad in the local newspaper announcing the start of the group and ended up with ten people who were interested in attending. From this random draw of people, all ten were artists! I don't know that there is an association between artists and people who have been hurt or abused, but this coincidental meeting of artists did seem to suggest that they were reaching out to others through their art as a way of being heard and understood. Our group consisted of a few writers, a painter, a poet, a few musicians, and an art gallery owner. We were amazed at the synchronicity of the group.

The experience in this group was compelling and powerful as the members came to understand and support each other. Not only did the strength and validation that they felt with each other help the members to heal and grow psychologically, but each person also became more productive in his or her artistic process. The members shared their artistic works with each other, appreciating the content of the feelings and experiences each expressed. But even more than this, they supported each other's creative process by deeply appreciating how they were each standing at the edge of themselves, stretching beyond their fears and pain into the unknown, becoming more fully alive all the while.

Through this group experience, I witnessed and felt the courage it took for people to face this pain, and I saw how the relationships among them served as the major source of strength in the creative process. I also noticed how the therapeutic process of healing and growth involved a creative element. These survivors were creating new selves, letting go of their injured identities in order to create a new life.

I also witnessed how the relationships within the group supported each person's capacity to engage in artistic creativity. This experience led me to specialize in creativity and to focus on the inner life of artists. I have worked with famous artists, not-so-famous artists, prolific artists, and blocked artists. Though very different in their backgrounds, their goals, and their talents, they all share similar struggles and similar fears. The intimacy of my psychotherapy relationships with these artists has allowed me to understand their inner experiences as they make their way through the creative process. I have come to respect artistic creation as one of the most challenging of all human activities. I owe my deepest gratitude to these artists who have invited me into their most personal and private spaces and have agreed to share their experiences. When I use examples from our sessions, of course I have changed names and other identifying information in order to protect their privacy and confidentiality.

This internal perspective unveils the artist's hopes and dreams as well as his fears and dreads, all of which impact his ability to stretch beyond his comfort zone so that he can dive into the creation of something new. This is the secret world of the artist, the innermost dimension of creative experience that I will share with you in this book.

In addition, I draw from my personal experiences and reflections. In examining my own struggles and blocks while writing this book, I find I have experienced many of them in a deeply personal, even painful way. Engaging, distancing, and reengaging in this process has confronted me with my own blocks and has stretched me past my comfort zone countless times.

Most books on creativity describe the creative process as a solitary and isolated endeavor. Creativity is something we do alone. It requires total engagement in the process. The creative state is one that is similar to a meditative trance, in that the artist becomes unaware of his or her surroundings and is free of external judgment and self-evaluation. This space has been called by such names as "flow," "the zone," and "focus." It is a state of intense focus and openness where imagination is free to roam and the entire self is poured into expression and creation. However, until now, the artist has been left on his own to somehow find and enter into this state.

Although the act of creation usually requires isolation from others, both in external reality and in internal awareness, I believe that the capacity to move in and out of this space is determined by the artist's experience of connectedness with others. Rather than understanding the ability to enter the creative space as evidence of the artist's sheer will, I will describe how certain kinds of relationships give her the strength and confidence to risk entering into this state. She can use her relationships with other people and other realms (such as spirituality, experiencing the art of another, loving, learning, and parenting) to strengthen and support herself. And, vice versa, she can use the strength she gains through the experience of creating to enhance her capacity to engage intimately with other people.

In effect, I would argue, the creative process involves the opposite of isolation and aloneness — it requires a capacity for *connection.* Viewing artistic blocks as understandable fears about connection can then help the artist identify what kinds of support he may need so that he can enter into a creative state. The nature of our relationships, whether they strengthen or deflate us, can determine our feelings of strength and safety to immerse in creativity. When we become aware of how our relationships affect our basic feelings of safety and trust, we can then try to elicit more of what we need from others to help us along in our creative process.

In addition, artists not only require certain kinds of relationships with other people in order to create, but they also require an intense connection with the art form itself. An artist's work is experienced both as an expression of himself and as a distinct "other" that he is playing with, interacting with, and being guided by. It is almost as if the artwork develops its own life. The artist and his artwork engage in a kind of relationship that propels both of them forward toward further definition and clarity.

Because I understand the creative process as deeply embedded in the experience of connection, I will call this creative state *immersion*. Creativity is a matter of immersing *into something* else so completely that one may feel, at times, entirely merged with (but also separate from) the artwork. My use of the word *immersion* is somewhat unique grammatically. Technically, it should be "immerse oneself in creativity," but I feel that, besides sounding rather awkward, that wording doesn't quite capture my meaning. I prefer to say, "one immerses into creativity," because I understand creativity as emerging from the play space between the artist and the artwork rather than as a solitary, internal state; this phrase seems to capture that meaning better.

The prospect of immersing into the creative space can be both exhilarating and terrifying. The artist hopes to experience a sense of meaning and purpose through her artistic expression and this hope propels her toward creative immersion. She hopes to heal parts of herself and to experience longed-for connections with others. But alongside these hopes she also fears she could be demolished or annihilated if she fails. For most artists, it takes tremendous courage and strength to risk immersion into creativity. It means letting go of self-protective defenses and diving into uncertainty and the unknown. The artist must let go of illusions of control. In this way, when anticipating creativity, the artist feels excited and enhanced but also vulnerable and unprotected.

I have found that many artists view their blocks to creativity as evidence of their weakness or defects: "If only I weren't so lazy," or "If only I weren't so distractible," or "I must not really want to succeed." My aim is to help artists appreciate that the creative process involves a natural ebb and flow in and out of immersive states. What may seem like being distracted or procrastination may actually be a productive phase of the overall process.

This book is organized into three parts. Part 1, The Secret World of Creativity, orients you to an internal perspective of the creative process. It provides the foundation of ideas for the rest of the book and explores the artist's inner experiences of hope and dread as she anticipates diving into a state of creative immersion. This part also describes universally experienced fears that can block our creative immersion and can increase the potential for experiencing psychological darkness throughout a project. I show how the creative process actually involves moving in and out of immersive states and how certain kinds of relationships with others can help you through the process.

Part 2, Relationships, describes the nature of these helpful relationships with others. I clarify the specific kinds of relationships you need to help you feel the hope and courage to complete a work of art. These types of relationships boost your confidence and strength so that you can continue to risk immersing into creativity. Another important relationship in the creative process is the one with the audience. I will show how your childhood and previous experiences lead you to certain assumptions about the audience and how these assumptions affect your creative work. I also describe how you can use deadlines to your advantage.

And part 3, Stages of the Creative Process, walks you through the psychological process from the start to the finish of an artistic project. I show how creativity actually consists of several distinct stages and how you can navigate through the process by making use of fantasy and real relationships with others. I describe the inner experience of creative immersion as well as the different kinds of feelings and events that cause us to disengage from immersion. No one can remain in an immersive state all the time. We naturally move between states of fusion with our artwork to states of disengagement from it. Periods of disengagement allow us to come back to ourselves, to step back from the immersive connection with the artwork in order to evaluate and craft it. And because immersive connections transform our inner selves, we come back to a new self that has been formed in the process.

This inevitable experience of disengagement from immersion is also the time when artists can become frustrated with themselves and with their project, and when they can be vulnerable to depression or other troubles. This type of negative experience during disengagement can expand into a more generalized feeling of psychological darkness. Because of this risk, I devote special attention to this stage and describe the various types of disengagement experiences you may have and ways to help you through them.

This book illuminates a dimension of our day-to-day experience that largely operates just outside of our awareness and yet exerts a powerful effect on our feelings, behaviors, and decisions. This dimension, of our sense of self-in-connection-with-others, is normally taken completely for granted and yet, when we shine a light on it, we discover what we are in need of to keep moving forward. Throughout the writing of this book, I was continually challenged to keep focused on artists' experiences as they made their way through the process of artistic creation. I say I was challenged because I kept finding myself straddling the ideas of artistic creation and creativity in general. Although I chose to focus on artistic creation, these ideas are easily extended to the process of creativity in all walks of life. Everyday life requires that we all become creative in some way: solving problems, creating new ideas, building new technologies, inventing new products, and the like. These acts of creation involve the same psychological challenges as those I have described for artists. I hope that readers who are every bit as creative but who do not call themselves artists can extend these ideas to their own circles of creativity.

Because the creative process ignites our innermost hopes, needs, fears, and dreads, it can be an exhilarating and challenging psychological experience. I firmly believe that understanding and respecting the fears and blocks involved in your creative process will help you to move through them. I have included a section called Guides at the end of most chapters to summarize the main points and to help you think about your particular circumstances. Because many of our blocks and assumptions about others are subconscious, I have developed a tool to help you get in touch with these, called Incomplete Sentence Prompts, included as an appendix. If you complete these sentences with the first thing that comes to your mind, you will likely see patterns emerge in your answers that can illuminate the unique nature of your hopes and fears. If you are interested in further reading, the bibliography includes sources for some of my background reading that extend beyond those works cited in this book.

My ultimate goal is to help you increase your self-empathy and to stir your curiosity about how artistic blocks are understandable and reasonable responses to your past experiences, your present fears, and your assumptions about the future. Once you are aware of how your blocks are actually your efforts at self-preservation, you can determine what you need from others to help you stretch beyond these fears.

In the end, it is not really how much willpower or self-discipline we have that determines our ability to enter into a creative state. When we find ourselves standing at water's edge, looking at the vast unknown and uncertainty involved in the creative process, it is our relationships with those around us that will empower or inhibit our dive.

PART ONE

The Secret World of Creativity

I really don't feel my poems are mine at all.
I didn't create them out of nothing.
I owe them to my relations with other people.

—— ROBERT GRAVES

When love and skill work together,
expect a masterpiece.

—— JOHN RUSKIN

CHAPTER ONE

The Challenge of Immersion

"... you must dive into the water."

"Alas," said he, "I have never learned to dive."

"There is nothing to learn," said she. "The art of diving is not to do anything new but simply to cease doing something. You have only to let yourself go."

"It is only necessary," said Vertue, with a smile, "to abandon all efforts at self-preservation."

"I think," said John, "that if it is all one, I would rather jump."

"It is not all one," said Mother Kirk. "If you jump, you will be trying to save yourself and you may be hurt. As well, you would not go deep enough. You must dive so that you can go right down to the bottom of the pool: for you are not to come up again on this side. There is a tunnel in the cliff, far beneath the surface of the water, and it is through that tunnel that you must pass so that you may come up on the far side."

— C. S. LEWIS, *THE PILGRIM'S REGRESS*

In this powerful passage, C. S. Lewis depicts the hope and dread of immersion. Although he was describing the challenge of immersing into spiritual faith, the passage also illustrates the internal challenge of the artist facing the creative process. Artists must delve into the unknown and live with the uncertainty that the creative process requires. But where does creativity come from? And how does an artist find the courage to dive into this unknown territory? Then, even after entry, what sustains an artist's ability to stay in this unknown place to be able to complete a work of art?

In order to answer the second two of these questions, which will ultimately help you along in your creative process, we must first understand where creativity comes from. We must begin with an understanding for what I have come to appreciate as the most fundamental and difficult challenge we face in creativity — finding the courage to enter into a creative state. Once we can acknowledge and respect this, then I can offer ideas about how to navigate through the process.

My fundamental assumption is that creativity (and the hope that is needed to fuel our forward movement) comes from a state of experience that I call *immersion*. The experience of immersion is one of total connection and engagement. Literally, to *immerse* means to plunge into something that surrounds or covers. We usually think of immersing into water: an immersed object is completely suspended in liquid but not drowned by it. Immersion means to be totally absorbed or engrossed in an activity.

It feels like simultaneously losing and finding the self. It is the experience of getting past our psychological boundaries and defenses and totally investing our heart and soul into something else. In creative activity, immersion means (in the current phrase) to be "in the zone," similar to being in a meditative trance in that the outside world melts away and new ideas, images, or sounds present themselves in a natural flow. Here, in this place, we experience ourselves in the fullest and most meaningful sense. This is where life exists, where fulfillment, gratification, and depth reside. Immersive moments are felt as soothing and energizing, relaxing and vitalizing.

We can think of immersion with another person, place, idea, or thing. We can experience immersive moments, or states, in a variety of realms. Let me offer a few examples of immersive experiences that generate hope, strength, and ultimately creativity:

> A young girl climbs up into her father's lap. She nestles in, big warm arms wrapped around her, the smell of sweet cologne lingering in his hours-old beard and the strength of his big, soft body encasing her. As with a warm fire on a cold night, she feels soothed, secure, and connected. She dreams of being a princess or a president. The future abounds with possibilities.
>
> A little boy stands at the sink beside his father. Dad armed with a razor, son holding a toothbrush, both stare into the mirror with tired eyes as they put shaving lotion on their cheeks. The little boy feels big, grown-up, and strengthened by this shared moment. Likewise, the father feels enhanced, gratified, and proud to be of such "use" to his son.
>
> A dancer listens to the music, initially thinking and planning what step will come next. "Will I have the strength and balance to attempt that move I did the other day?" Then, swept away into the motion of the music, she moves and turns without thought. Without a plan but always with a grasp — a hold on the rhythm and the verse — she gets lost in the beauty and finds her own grace.
>
> Wrapped in deep thought and with books piled all around, he gets an inkling of an idea. He stops, paralyzed and afraid to move lest he lose his train of thought. Then, almost magically, the idea builds upon itself, new formulations, and new connections. He'll write them down later — better now to ride this intellectual tide to see where it may take him.

We all long for experiences of immersion. We seek them in many realms: our relationships, our work, our art, our spirituality. There is no denying the powerful and profound sense of meaning and purpose immersive moments provide. Often, we wait for them to happen. When by chance they do, we grab hold of them as precious gems of life — and often we feel sustained and energized by them for long periods afterward.

Of course, we can and do engage in our activities without the experience of immersion. A dancer I know described a profound shift in her feelings about herself when she was in an immersive state during dance compared to when she was not. When she was immersed in dance, she experienced herself as graceful and beautiful. She confidently moved across the floor, feeling enhanced by her movements. However, at other times, when she was not immersed and was, instead, "on the outside of the dance," she experienced herself as inadequate and self-conscious. She compared herself to other dancers, concluding that her body type was "not right." She focused on her technical flaws and found that she would trip herself up by thinking too much about what she was doing. As she alternated between these immersive and nonimmersive states, her self-perception and experience changed completely. Thus, it is not the activity, per se, that generates immersion, but the doer's internal state and engagement that define it.

Immersive moments propel us forward into transformation and change; we are enhanced and strengthened in the connection. From this enhanced state, new forms, conceptions, and thoughts emerge. This is the psychological-spiritual-intuitive edge of the self where creative imagination exists.

It is interesting to consider that the experience of immersion serves a healing and vitalizing function: the artistic product emerging from the immersive experience is itself often not the artist's goal. The experience of immersion can feel like a sense of home. In fact, immersion can be a self-consolidating state, a place to go when we feel worn down or fragile.

I have heard many artists describe their work as a fundamental need. One composer said that he could not go for more than a few days (actually he found ten was his limit) before he just "had to write music." He felt a driving need to express himself. But could it also be that he needed the immersive experience he found during composing to sustain his sense of wholeness, completeness, and vitality? In later chapters, I discuss how the experience of immersion is actually a crucial element in psychological health as well as in the creative process.

Evidence that immersive experience is psychologically sustaining and restorative is reflected in our attempts to schedule and structure its possible occurrence. Attending church services or psychotherapy sessions on a weekly basis can be quite sustaining. Perhaps, too, the idea of a regularly planned date night with one's spouse is a wish for a regular immersive experience.

Yet as wonderful as this immersive experience is, it can also be very frightening to allow it. A strong sense of dread parallels the hopeful promise of immersion. To allow immersion requires taking a leap of faith into uncertainty and vulnerability. Most of us find it frightening to consider taking this leap into the unknown as our trust in others, ourselves, and the world has been chipped away at (or traumatically obliterated) in the course of life. The sense of abandon — the giving up of reins of control, familiarity, and self-protective defenses — required for these immersive moments can be truly terrifying. There is no guarantee of the outcome. Opening to immersion requires sitting still with uncertainty. Its product and process are unknown. To experience the immersive connection that generates creativity, one must recklessly and without defense dive into the water, letting go of conscious control and manipulation. Our entire being can feel at risk of demolishment. Many of us choose (consciously or unconsciously) not to dive, which protects our vulnerable selves but diminishes our sense of being fully alive and connected.

IMMERSIVE REALMS

Immersion can be experienced in most areas of life. I'd like to describe various realms of possible immersive experience to help you get the feel for how central this idea is to our day-to-day functioning. And beyond the general interest of viewing parts of our lives through a new lens, later I describe how you can also use your immersive experiences in these other realms to help you along in the creative process.

Artistic Expression

A famous photographer spoke of her inner shift, from control to immersion, in her approach to taking pictures. She described her early career in photography as consisting of the hard work of "making pictures." She put a lot of energy into finding and creating the perfect shot. Then she came to rely on and trust the process of immersion; she began "waiting for the pictures to present themselves to her." This approach, albeit much more uncertain and out of her control, freed her artistic energy, and she began discovering many more gripping scenes.

Many artists have reported that they will often have immersive moments, giving rise to creative ideas, in that state between wakefulness and sleep. Perhaps this is understandable, because in that space, a person's psychological defenses are down. The mind is less inhibited by fear and, as it enters the sleep and dream world, is more relaxed and open. Many artists report keeping a pen and paper bedside in order to record these ideas so that they are not covered over again by conscious control.

One distinction worth mentioning here is that between creating audience-driven art, or making something prescribed by audience demand, and creating something new from the inside. Rollo May, a psychologist who has written extensively about creativity, also looked to the inner experience of the artist to define true creativity. In his book

The Courage to Create he distinguished "genuine creativity" from "escapist creativity." He understood genuine creativity as involving an act of encounter, an idea similar to that of immersion. He defined encounter as an inner experience of intensity, absorption, and engagement. On the other hand, he writes, "escapist creativity is that which lacks encounter"; it is performed for purposes other than self-reintegration or "engagement in encounter." Creating only for purposes of wealth, fame, or recognition can lack the experiential component of encounter which propels new forms of self-integration to emerge.

Everyone agrees that making art involves self-expression. However, I suggest that genuine creativity involves much more. It involves the artist immersing in the art form, which then invites the audience into that immersive space. Creativity reaches for connection. This ability of the artist to create an immersive experience with her audience is what defines a gripping work of art. Talented artists have a way of inviting others into their immersive realm. Picasso described his experience of painting:

> A picture is not thought out and settled beforehand. While it is being done it changes as one's thoughts change. And when it is finished, it still goes on changing, according to the state of mind of whoever is looking at it. A picture lives a life like a living creature, undergoing the changes imposed on us by our life from day to day. This is natural enough, as the picture lives only through the man who is looking at it.

In fact, another way to experience immersion is by appreciating someone else's art. I believe that it is the hope for an immersive experience that leads us to art galleries, concerts, and bookstores. Listening to music, looking at a painting or photograph, watching a ballet, or reading a book can be a vitalizing, strengthening, and transformative experience. Carl Rotenberg referred to this immersive experience as a "shared experiential space" between the viewer and the artist. We feel that the artist has expressed what we needed to express, that the artist has put into form what we experience and imagine. In my words, we feel immersed with the artist and immersed with the artwork. Another description of this experience comes from Gaston Bachelard in *Poetics of Space*, describing his experience reading poetry:

> The image offered us by reading the poem now becomes really our own. It takes root in us. It has been given to us by another, but we begin to have the impression that we could have created it, that we should have created it. It becomes a new being in our language, expressing us by making us what it expresses; in other words, it is at once a becoming of expression and a becoming of our being.

When we immerse in someone else's art, we find our own creativity. This immersive experience inspires us to be creative in our own way. I experience this when listening to certain music. I am swept up in it: I notice my heart beating faster, a flurry of energy and anticipation building inside of me, and a desire swelling to make my own art. I am a dancer, and in these immersive moments I either fantasize dancing or actually get up and spontaneously choreograph a dance. Interestingly, I also find that listening to music and dancing mobilizes my creativity in academic and intimacy realms. I have often come up with new intellectual ideas while dancing, as well as feeling more connected with my loved ones.

Most people seem to recognize this phenomenon, at least at some level. Many artists describe a need to "feed" on others' art when they feel their own creative energy lacking. In order to sustain their own creative process, they need to find immersive moments offered through the art of another. Later, I develop this idea even further by describing how finding alternative immersive experiences is necessary to sustaining our own creative productivity.

Intimate Relationships

The experience of new love epitomizes immersion in the realm of intimate relationships. When couples first fall in love, they tend to swim in immersive states together. There is often a profound sense of connection; they feel fulfilled in a lifelong desire to be completely understood and held. People describe the bliss of finding their soul mate, a person they feel totally connected with and almost as one with. There is usually complete trust in this space. People can be quite creative and productive during this time, as they feel enhanced and their hope for the future is bright. It is an energizing time, full of immersive experiences, which most people anticipate and recall as the best life has to offer.

This high usually moderates over time as reality and individual differences crack the immersive bubble. Perhaps the biggest challenge that couples face over time is sustaining immersive moments with each other. Although it is difficult to replicate the intensity of first-love immersion, couples often find a deeper and more firmly grounded sense of immersive experience with each other. These immersive states are experienced through mutual empathy, shared life experiences, and shared emotional moments.

Sexual intimacy is also a powerful immersive experience. Through sexual intimacy, people feel totally engrossed, engulfed in one another, as one. Of course, emotional intimacy can enhance sexual immersion and vice versa.

Many people are frightened of emotional intimacy and turn to sexual intimacy for their sense of immersion with their partner. Sex becomes a crucial element in their sense of connectedness. Without sexual immersion, these people tend to feel isolated and alone. When the fear of emotional intimacy is extreme, sexual addictions can develop. These people are desperate for experiences of immersion, and they turn to frequent casual sexual encounters or other sexual activities to temporarily get their fix of immersion.

Likewise, some people are afraid of immersing sexually. Sexual dysfunctions, lack of sexual desire, and sexual inhibitions are often symptoms of the deeper fear of being vulnerable and hurt if immersion is allowed. In general, people are in search of immersive experiences with each other. However, many people do not feel safe enough or trusting enough to allow this level of vulnerability and uncertainty. There are no guarantees in love, and many people are too frightened to let down their self-protective shields to allow immersion with another and will compensate for this lack of experience through a variety of efforts.

It is important to distinguish immersive experiences that lead to creativity and hope from nonproductive or empty immersive experiences that numb and diminish feelings and experience. Examples of nonproductive immersion include the use of drugs or alcohol, involvement in cults, compulsive overeating, and attachments to abusive relationships. Each of these can offer the user a temporary experience of immersion but can also lead to addictions and other problems. In her book *Creating the Capacity for Attachment: Treating Addictions and the Alienated Self*, Karen Walant explores how addictions can serve to temporarily fill the person's need for immersion when he has basically given up on experiencing immersive moments with others due to repeated disappointments and failures. Usually, one who is vulnerable to such activities is horribly lacking in the experience of immersion in other areas of his or her life. Although drugs, cults, eating, TV, and the like can temporarily fulfill this need to blend into something else, they often rob the person of his sense of uniqueness and leave him feeling more lost than before. In fact, many psychological symptoms and disorders can be traced to the absence of immersive moments, both in childhood development and in adult life. Symptoms such as depression, anxiety, and addictions exist as evidence of this absence or as attempts to create it.

Psychotherapy

Although they may not be aware of it, people who seek psychotherapy are seeking an immersive experience. Even if a person enters therapy with a wish to solve a specific problem, the "cure" of therapy lies in the relationship between therapist and client. The hope that brings a person to psychotherapy is that she will be completely understood and validated in a way that she has not experienced before. There is a hope for a new beginning. She hopes to connect with a powerful "other" who will be understanding and responsive and through this connection to find her pain and suffering alleviated.

The dread that usually accompanies this hopeful expectation is that she will, once again, be hurt or disappointed. She dreads that previous painful experiences with others will be repeated with the therapist and that she will again feel alone and misunderstood. She dreads that she will be labeled, judged, and perceived only from the outside and not understood or appreciated in that perception.

People tend to enter psychotherapy with this parallel experience: the hope for immersive experience and the dread either that it won't happen or that they will be hurt if they allow it. No wonder so many people resist treatment! Appreciating this dilemma leads to the conclusion that the most important approach psychotherapists can use is empathy. To have empathy means to perceive a person from the inside out, to put oneself in another's shoes and find the sense in their feelings, thoughts, and behaviors. Through empathic encounters, immersive connections can ultimately diminish feelings of aloneness while strengthening the person's core. Given that I am writing to artists, rather than therapists, how can this understanding be useful to you? I believe one of your major tasks in moving through the creative process is finding a way to be more empathic with your own experience. When you are hitting an artistic block, it is more helpful to try to understand the sense of the block (what fears are sensibly keeping you from taking the dive?) rather than to beat yourself up by labeling yourself as lazy or unmotivated or inadequate.

You can become more of an understanding presence to yourself if you take a stance of empathic curiosity about what fears you are rightly experiencing and what kind of support you need to boost your confidence. There are a variety of psychological theories that explain human behavior and psychotherapeutic cure: psychodynamic, behavioral, cognitive, existential, family systems, and others. Although different in their focus and techniques, all have been shown to be helpful. One unifying way to understand how these different approaches can all work is through the idea of immersion. Each approach understands the client in a different way. However, each is fundamentally based on the quality of the relationship between therapist and patient. Because each promises the hope of immersive experience in the relationship, the language that the theory uses does not matter much. Good therapy, regardless of approach, involves reaching for understanding and connection with the client.

Spirituality

Many people experience immersion through spiritual or religious practice. As with psychotherapy, there are many types of religions. But the common element in all religions is the promise of immersion with a higher power, whether that is God, nature, or humanity. As with anything else, a person can engage in religious rituals without an experience of immersion. And vice versa, a person can experience spiritual immersion without practicing a particular religion. Again, it is the internal experience the person brings to the religion that defines it as immersive or not.

Spirituality is fundamentally built on faith and trust. Mystical experience — or the experience of being "born again," or of communicating with God, or of being enlightened — derives from immersive experience. Immersing with a higher power is strengthening and vitalizing.

Play

Immersion is clearly demonstrated in children at play. Adults often watch children play with wonder and amazement. Witnessing children's capacity to totally immerse in playful activities, alone and with others, delights us. Children can slip in and out of immersive states with ease: they have not yet built a repertoire of disappointments and humiliations that lead to psychological defensiveness and fears that inhibit immersion. So they can play without self-consciousness, free to delve into fantasy worlds and imagination. I used to watch my young son with amazement and awe as he created fantastic worlds with himself in them, spinning off dialogues and story lines as if no one was watching. He played in a space that incorporated both fantasy and reality. And often, he would invite me into this space to play along with him. In my good moments, I could go there with him and immerse in the moment, careful not to intrude with reality or corrections. His freedom to create in these spaces fascinated me. I knew that, above all else, this was the most important aspect of his experience. I suppose that the essence of my parenting approach has been to try to respect and preserve (as much as is possible as a parent) his freedom to immerse.

The play space is a transitional space between fantasy and reality, between known and unknown, between old and new, and between people. Humor happens here. Expression happens here. And the sense that life is worth living happens here.

Learning

To learn something new means to confront the edge between what is already known and what is *not* known. Oliver Wendell Holmes once said, "A man's mind, once stretched by a new idea, never regains its original dimensions." In many ways, learning is similar to creating in that the learner must be willing to let go of old forms so that new forms can exist. Learning something new can dismantle a person's existing knowledge structures, which have been comfortably in place. Being open to new learning requires more than a willingness to supplement existing material. It can mean a total reconfiguration and reorganization of previous understandings.

We face threats in learning that are similar to those in other immersive activities. Our self-perceptions of being competent and smart can be challenged ("Why didn't I think of that?" or "I thought I was an expert"). Furthermore, in the Western tradition of education, testing and evaluation are often the primary goal of learning. Our school systems place emphasis on passing tests rather than on immersing in learning. The student is continually threatened with external observation and evaluation. This performance-based focus calls up anxiety and defensiveness and often inhibits (or at least does not encourage) immersive engagement in learning. Rote memorization and learning toward the goal of passing a test do not challenge reorganization of existing meaning structures. Information and ideas are not integrated — they are merely tagged onto short-term memory and are quickly forgotten once the test is over. On the other hand, meaningful interaction and immersion with new material propel new structures and understandings of experience to emerge.

Parenting

I believe that immersive experiences are the most important thing we can make available to our children. Babies have a natural need for immersion. They reach to be held, cry to be responded to, and engage in communicative efforts even from day one. When these needs are met, more often than not, parent and child experience mutual gratification through immersive moments with each other. But even more important, development and growth occur in these spaces. In the same way that creativity and hope are generated through immersion, so are physical, psychological, social, and cognitive maturation and development.

In our culture, it is much easier to validate and respond to an infant's need for immersive closeness than when the child gets older. Most parents are happy to respond to the baby's needs for physical closeness and connection. However, as the child ages, we become concerned that we will spoil him and make him dependent on us by responding to him. This hesitancy to allow immersion with our children comes, in part, from psychology and the idea that frustrating the child's needs for attachment and connection leads to the development of independence and autonomy. These views assume that independence and autonomy are the goal of development. Many parenting handbooks recommend letting a baby cry himself to sleep so that he will not become dependent on the soothing arms of the parent to fall asleep. The parent's fear is that if a child comes to depend on immersive moments to regulate her needs, she will never learn to self-regulate. The child will be forever dependent upon the parents, never separating or developing an independent identity.

This is one example of disengagement from our children. For many parents, it does not feel intuitively right. Yet, because they strive to be good parents, they force themselves to resist immersing with their child "for the child's own good." One parenting manual I read addressed this dilemma and actually made the suggestion that parents turn on the vacuum cleaner to drown out the noise of their crying child if it got to be too painful to listen to.

Thank goodness our psychological understandings about the nature of growth and development are becoming more sophisticated. Contemporary infant research is finding that quite the opposite of this notion holds true, in both physical and psychological development. Babies flourish physically when they are held. Babies who are not held fail to thrive. Similarly, psychological growth and development occur within relationships, not apart from them. In fact, current theories challenge the fundamental assumption that independence and autonomy are the goals of maturity. In our present culture, people seem to have a much more difficult time *attaching* with others than being independent. Perhaps because we were raised for generations under the assumption that "for our own good" we should not rely on others for responsiveness to our needs (needing immersive experiences is bad or weak), what we really learned was that others could not be trusted to respond to us and we gave up. We instead learned to turn to pacifiers, then thumbs, then drugs to be soothed. And we wonder why the neurosis of our generations is a sense of emptiness, aloneness, and addiction.

IMMERSING INTO CREATIVITY

Through interviews and hundreds of hours of psychotherapy I've had with artists, one common thread in their descriptions of the creative process is the need for immersing in the art without regard to external or internal evaluation. As I have described, this involves a total investment of the self. It is a matter of getting past the "observing eye" — either internally imposed or perceived in the audience. In this state, artists describe feeling "cohesive," "whole," "totally integrated," and "complete."

Jackson Pollock described his technique and immersive experience while painting:

> On the floor I am more at ease. I feel nearer, more a part of the painting, since this way I can walk around it, work from the four sides and literally be in the painting.... When I am in my painting, I'm not aware of what I am doing. It is only after a sort of "getting acquainted" period that I see what I have been about. I have no fears about making changes, destroying the

image, etc., because the painting has a life of its own. I try to let it come through. It is only when I lose contact with the painting that the result is a mess. Otherwise there is pure harmony, an easy give and take, and the painting comes out well.

However, these immersive states must then be followed by stepping back from the internal experience. In this more detached state, the artist examines, evaluates, and manipulates his work. This is the state where he assesses and tweaks the content and form of the work. Outside of the immersive connection, the artist considers the adequacy of his work and how others will perceive it. It is in this stage of the creative process that the artist is vulnerable to feelings of self-doubt, inadequacy, and insecurity. The previously experienced wholeness in immersion can be broken apart. The artist may retreat from the work as a form of self-preservation against these feelings, and he may feel depressed, anxious, and hopeless.

The psychological process of creativity involves this internal movement from states of immersion (where the artist feels whole and complete) to states of disengagement (where the artist evaluates his work and can feel threatened by judgment) to states of reengagement (where the artist feels able to reinvest in his work with renewed energy.) Heinz Kohut, the father of the contemporary theory known as Self Psychology, described this internal experience of creativity: "Creative people tend to alternate during periods of productivity between phases when they think extremely highly of their work and phases when they are convinced that it has no value."

If the artist feels weak or inadequate during the period of disengagement from his creative immersion, he needs to turn to an alternative realm of immersion (such as a sustaining relationship, spirituality, play, etc.) to restore his energy, hope, and strength. If he can experience immersive connection in another realm, he will again feel strong enough, repaired enough, to reengage his creative connection with the artwork.

Perhaps that sounds simple, but for many reasons that I will out-line in the chapters to come, it is easier said than done. The fears that surface when confronting this task can seem overwhelming and insurmountable. But certain kinds of relationships with others can enable us to get beyond the inevitable fears that occur throughout the creative process. The three fundamental types of relationships we need to be at our best can be designated as mirrors, heroes, and twins. Mirrors are people who reflect us: they see our strengths, our unique-ness, and our talents and strengthen us by appreciating what we have to offer. Heroes are people we look up to and admire; they inspire us to reach beyond our safety zones. Twins are people who are in the same boat and comfort us by sharing similar struggles and triumphs. These relationships serve as solid foundations from which to dive into creativity. Because these relationships play such a vital role in the creative process, I will describe them in detail in part 2. But for now, let's take a closer look at the nature of certain universal fears that we all face regarding immersion.

UNIVERSAL FEARS

Some of the fears that block immersion are universally experienced, familiar to people across cultures and across generations. Symbolic representations of these fears are found throughout art and literature, theology, psychology, and philosophy:

THE FEAR OF LETTING GO. We can liken the state of immersion to that of a trapeze artist suspended in midair between two trapeze bars. To catch the next one, I must let go of the previous one. Once I let go, I have no choice but to reach forward. Or drop. In grabbing the next bar, I discard the old one and end up in a new place. The state of sus-pension, the gap between the old and the new, is terrifying. What if there is nothing to grab hold of and the old is gone forever?

THE FEAR OF LOSS OF CONTROL. There is safety in familiarity. With a known entity, I have the illusion of control. Because immersion means I must allow for uncertainty and the unknown, I fear being powerless and lost in this unknown territory.

THE FEAR OF ANNIHILATION. The forfeiture of control in immersive states can be felt as a threat to one's entire self. Most of us need a firm grasp on our sense (illusion) of control over ourselves and our environment. We feel safe and organized when things are going as planned. But to let go of this illusion of self-protection can leave us feeling at risk of being demolished. It provokes a fear of chaos and disorganization: "I could die if I let go."

THE FEAR OF EMOTIONS. If I allow immersion, I might experience emotions that are overwhelming and uncontrollable. Painful feelings are particularly frightening. What if I open a Pandora's box of pain and suffering, and I can't close it again? What emotions lurk deep inside of me that I'm not aware of? Particularly in Western culture, emotionality is often devalued: giving in to emotions is perceived as weak or self-serving. This has led many people to feel ashamed of their feelings, and they have become experts at suppressing and hiding their emotions. This leaves them fearing a flood of unknown and unwanted feelings. They fear that if they allow immersion, the emergent feelings will be overwhelming and uncontrollable: "I might go insane."

You may experience any or all of these fears, either consciously or unconsciously, when facing immersion. Although there is no easy way to get past these fears, identifying their presence can help you make sense of your anxiety and resistance to immersion. The rest of this book will help you identify what you need to get beyond these fears — in particular, as noted, you will see that certain kinds of relationships with others (mirrors, heroes, and twins) can help you past blocks to immersion.

IMMERSING INTO HOPE

Where do we get the strength to dive into creative immersion despite these fears? Through hope. And where does hope come from? Hope also comes from immersion. In the same magical way that creativity is generated in immersive experience, hope is also generated in this space.

Hope is a complex blend of wishes and needs, and a longing for magical transformation. Hope points toward the future. In extreme cases, it signifies that there even *is* a future. When we have hope, we are able to meet challenges with vigor and energy. It propels us forward. Hope pulls us through even the worst of times.

Without hope, we experience apathy or despair. I am reminded of a story told to me by Anna Ornstein, MD, a renowned child psychiatrist who is also a Holocaust survivor. She was detained at Auschwitz from the age of fourteen to seventeen. Reflecting on her experiences there, she recalled a striking distinction between people who were able to retain hope and those who fell into despair. Those who had hope fared better physically and psychologically. Those filled with despair withered: they gave up and died, physically or psychologically.

She concluded that the difference between the hopeful and the hopeless was creativity. The Nazis must have known this, because creativity was strictly prohibited in the concentration camps: those found to be writing or singing or drawing were severely punished, if not killed. But those prisoners who secretly found a way to create seemed to retain a sense of hope. She was so struck with this difference that, sixty years later, she concludes that creativity kept many people alive and sane.

Where does hope come from? It seems so vital, so crucial to our existence and yet so abstract and indefinable. I believe it grows out of immersion. The Holocaust victims who could still find immersive moments retained hope. Anna herself described feeling "lucky," "much better off," than most of the others because her mother was detained with her. She described frequent immersive experiences with her mother, which helped her to hold on to a sense of hopefulness for their future.

Another example of finding hope in immersion comes to mind. A woman I had been seeing in psychotherapy fell into a state of despair after a series of losses and major stress. She felt she could not go on and for the first time in her life felt suicidal. All of her hope was gone. She could not see or feel anything but pain. Everything was dark. Rather than trying to convince her that she had a better future, or reassuring her, or even being frightened of her despair (which would have led me to take control and hospitalize her), I sat in the darkness with her. I had to trust that if we could immerse together in her pain, she could find the strength to go on.

In order to immerse with me, she would need to trust my capacity to immerse with her and to understand her. Expressing oneself entails a certain level of trust and hope of being heard. If a person does not anticipate being heard or understood, he or she will not risk self-expression.

Because of our history together, my client trusted me to be understanding of her experience. She articulated how despairing she felt. She described her sense of intolerable pain and grief. She was able to put into words the relentless agony that pervaded her life. I sat there with her, imagining what it would be like to be in her shoes, understanding and appreciating her pain. I did not try to fix it or cure her or pull her into a different mind-set. We sat there, both in that emotional darkness — together. We were immersed with each other.

Out of the darkness, a flicker of light sparked for her. And it grew large enough that even she was surprised. A flicker of hope. Out of the dark. But we had to sit there together, quietly, patiently, waiting for it and not knowing if it would come.

In general, immersing in pain, whether it is in a therapeutic relationship or a parent-child relationship or a relationship with a work of art, is very difficult. We fear that immersing in the pain will make it worse and that we will be swallowed up in it if we allow it expression. However, sometimes hope can be reached only through immersion in that prolonged and terrifying dread. T. S. Eliot wrote a powerful poetic description of this seeming paradox:

> I said to my soul, be still, and wait without hope
> For hope would be hope for the wrong thing...
> Wait without thought, for you are not ready for thought:
> So the darkness shall be the light, and the stillness the dancing.

Out of immersion come creativity and hope. Hope for a new beginning and creative ideas about how to bring it about. This hope and creativity do not lie preformed in a person. They are generated in the immersive space between self and other. Again, here we find the leading edge of the human spirit.

GUIDES

I. MAKE IMMERSION THE GOAL.

Rather than focusing on production or performance, focus on having an immersive experience. In other words, if you reach toward accomplishment, you are keeping your experience on an external, evaluative plane. Because you are observing yourself and judging your performance based on external measures, fears of inadequacy or failure are more likely to surface. By switching your focus to internal experience, you are more likely to find a path to your creativity.

Because immersing means letting go of self-protective defenses and involves facing the unknown, try to adopt an attitude of *curiosity*. What will be generated from this experience of immersion? What will evolve? Where will it take me? You may decide later not to include the result in the project, but be curious to see what, if anything, is generated this time. With this perspective, it is almost like being in the audience of a show that is about to begin. It becomes a curious anticipation of the unknown, and today you will allow the immersive experience to do the creating.

2. ACCEPT MOVEMENT IN AND OUT OF IMMERSION.

Know and accept that movement in and out of immersive states is normal, natural, and part of the overall process. Stop blaming and criticizing yourself when you are not immersed. Disengagement is a necessary part of creation. You must rest and reorganize after an immersive experience. Because immersion generates a "new you," you must periodically step back to integrate the new experience. Learn to relax and accept that states of disengagement can be psychologically difficult. Every artist experiences them; you are not alone.

3. ENGAGE IN ALTERNATIVE REALMS OF IMMERSION.

Experiences of immersion are strengthening and enhancing no matter where they occur. Immersion in artistic pursuits is but one realm of possible immersive experience. Other possible realms include intimate relationships, spirituality, experiencing other art, new learning, parenting, psychotherapy, athletic pursuits, and play. When you have a healthy balance of potential immersive realms, you will naturally flow in and out of connection in different realms. This process of flowing among different types of connections enhances your capacity to immerse in any one realm. When you disengage from immersion in your artwork and need regeneration and strengthening, you can turn to immersive connection in another realm and experience the support and comfort there that you need to reenter artistic immersion. And so on and so on.

The development and pursuit of other immersive experiences is not a distraction. It is often a vital and necessary part of sustaining an artistic endeavor. In addition, it is often through these varied pursuits that we develop a solid support system of appreciative others where we get many of our psychological needs for connection met — not to mention that we find increased fulfillment and meaning in our lives when we have multiple realms in which to experience immersion.

CHAPTER TWO

The Light and Dark of Immersion

Destruction of the world that we have built and in which we
live, and of ourselves within it; but then a wonderful reconstruction of the bolder, cleaner, more spacious, and fully human
life — that is the lure, the promise and the terror... that we
carry within.

— JOSEPH CAMPBELL,
THE HERO WITH A THOUSAND FACES

Here's how the struggle to immerse often works: I knew I wanted
to write a section about hope for chapter 1. I kept delaying sitting down to write (I had so many chores to accomplish first!) because
I didn't have concrete ideas about what to say. I had a general notion
about the essence of immersion and hope, but I hadn't defined the
words or the outline. "OK, it's time now, just sit down and see what
comes out," I said to myself, trying to heed my own words. I realized
that I feared I was diving into an unknown and very uncertain place.
I was afraid that I would feel totally disorganized and discouraged if
I trusted the process and only became more confused. My entire sense
of adequacy was on the line. I drew a breath and I started. Seemingly
from nowhere, I remembered the conversation with Anna Ornstein.
I had not thought about that discussion in years — and I certainly had

not planned to incorporate it to illustrate hope. But there it was. It organized me and it gave me hope. So I went with it — finding a path as I went. It formed. It evolved. I experienced immersion.

We must find the courage to immerse into creativity not just once but a hundred, even a thousand, times throughout an artistic project. Immersion is a fluid, changing experience that depends on many factors. On some days it is easy to immerse. In fact, it may feel uncomfortable *not* to immerse in the project. And on other days taking the plunge may be the most difficult thing in the world. Additionally, some projects may be easier to immerse with than others. If we understand that the creative process involves moving in and out of immersive states, then we can explore the various reasons why it is more or less difficult to immerse at any one point in time.

Although artistic blocks occur for a variety of reasons, understanding them is the first step toward getting past them. If we do not recognize the nature of the blocks and find ways to move through them, we are at risk of getting stuck in a state of unproductive disengagement. In this chapter I will describe the darkness that many artists experience (including depression, anxiety, and addictions) when they get stuck and cannot find an alternative source of immersion.

The following is a story of a woman who struggled with sustaining immersion while writing a novel and who was able to use our therapy relationship to help herself. As you will see, her blocks to immersion occurred at various points and for various reasons, and she regularly needed to turn to her connection with me to be able to reenter her immersion in writing.

LONGING FOR A LOVE STORY

Jane began psychotherapy with me in hope of getting past writer's block. She began by saying that she was working on her fourth novel.

Her second novel had received professional acclaim and had won many awards, and her third novel became a bestseller. She had suddenly arrived at fame and fortune. Her publisher paid her half a million dollars to begin her next book. Although she worked diligently on the first few chapters, she ended up throwing it all out because she felt it lacked the "magic" she had created in the previous books.

Now she was stuck. Paralyzed. She was unable to write and unable to generate new ideas. She reasoned that her block was due to the huge amount of money she was being paid to write the book; she felt an enormous pressure to meet her publisher's and readers' expectations.

She went on to say that she believed she had a more serious problem. She interpreted her writer's block as an "unconscious self-defeating" aspect of her personality. She saw her current paralysis as evidence of self-sabotage — that somewhere inside herself, she wanted to fail. When I asked her if she felt a conscious wish to fail, she said, "No. In fact, I've tried very hard in my life to achieve, and I feel that my dream to be a successful writer is finally coming true." It didn't appear to me that she would be trying to sabotage her own efforts, even unconsciously.

What we immediately distinguished was her experience in writing this book from that in writing the others. Here, she could not find her immersive space, from which her previous books had been generated. She could not find "the zone." Now, with fame and expectation, she was focused on, and stressed by, her audience. "Will this be believable?" "What does the audience want?" "Will this be as good as the last books?" "Will this book be worth this huge amount of money?" "Will my publisher be disappointed?" We understood that the external pressure she was feeling inhibited her capacity to immerse in the writing, in the story, and in the characters.

The nature of her block became clearer as she described her childhood. Her father had been verbally and physically abusive to her throughout her youth. Even today, he was critical and had never read even one of her books. Never one to support or encourage, he would instead belittle her: "You're never going to amount to anything," "You'd be lucky if any man would have you," "You're stupid, although you think you're smart." Despite her obvious intellect and creative talent, she suffered from low self-esteem and had always doubted her capacities. Her writing had been her escape. Here, she could create stories of great romance and adventure and identify with the main heroine as beautiful and smart.

We came to understand that when confronted with an audience, her deep, fundamental assumption was that they, like her father, were hostile and would be critical and devaluing (despite the acclaim and popularity she had received). It made sense that she would be frightened of immersing herself in a project that would result in a critical, hostile response. Her block was not self-sabotage; it was self-preservation!

Once we made this shift in understanding her block and she could consciously and rationally differentiate her audience from her father, she felt a great deal of relief. She and I also experienced an instant sense of connection with each other. We managed to experience an immersive moment of understanding even within that first session. Time flew by (as is usually the experience in immersive states) and the session ended.

She returned the following week, bright, energized, and grateful. She had experienced a flurry of ideas, typing so fast she could hardly keep up with what seemed to be "entire, complete chapters, already formed, waiting to be transcribed." Her publisher was ecstatic, affirming, "This has the magic," but my patient already knew that.

As one might expect, however, this was not a complete resolution. Jane had further episodes of writer's block followed by self-devaluation and self-loathing. Her next block occurred after a couple of weeks of uninterrupted writing. She described being immersed in the story, following her imagination into romance and fantasy. She recalled a particular moment, when, "stopping for a breath," she became aware of how much she had forgotten about her audience. A wave of panic engulfed her: she felt tremendously exposed, overexposed really, aware of how vulnerable she was making herself, how she lacked protective boundaries. The creative flow shut down. She felt naked, bare, and without any kind of protection. Again, she turned to the psychotherapy relationship for an experience of immersion. As I understood her experience of what it would be like to feel so exposed and why it made sense that she would feel a need to cover up, she found this shared understanding quite strengthening and was able to return to writing.

Another interesting block occurred when the content of what she was writing became frightening. In her immersed state, she created deeply complex characters and brought an intense love story to life. The intimacy shared by her characters was far deeper than any she had experienced in her own life. In fact, after a failed marriage, she had isolated herself from others out of fear of betrayal and disappointment. In her immersive space through writing, she could bring to the page her longed-for intimate connection with a man. However, in the midst of this fictional relationship, she was confronted with her own fears of hurt and disappointment. These fears grabbed her out of her immersion in the story. She was overcome with feelings of loss and failure and a sense of her own inadequacy in finding intimacy with others. She turned to me with an aching need to be understood and emotionally held. After several sessions where we understood and appreciated her fears, she was restored enough to return to the characters and continue their story of deep, immersive love.

Of course, this episode of anxiety and depression helped us to appreciate her isolation from others and to clarify her wish to find a way to engage in an intimate relationship again. We were able to draw on the strength she found periodically in her writing to help her reach out to others in real life. This process of moving back and forth between realms of immersion with her artistic activity, with me, and with her cat (many people readily find immersive experiences with pets) helped her to sustain her artistic productivity as well as to boost her courage in risking intimate connection with others. She completed her fourth book, and it received even greater acclaim than her previous ones.

Being blocked and then reengaging with work, as was Jane's experience, is part of the creative process. What Jane saw as a failure or defect in herself (self-defeating behavior) could instead be viewed as an understandable, self-preserving defense against her fear of being broken apart through criticism. Once she could understand the sensibility of the fears that blocked her artistic immersion, she could accept them as parts of her overall creative process and recognize that she needed positive support from others to overcome her feelings of inadequacy.

Jane's capacity to immerse was blocked by her fear of failure, her fear of a hostile audience, her fear of being overexposed, and her distrust of others. It seemed that being able to immerse with me in the therapy strengthened her and restored her sense of courage so that she could reengage with her writing with hope and openness. Finding alternative realms of immersion was a necessary part of her ability to complete her book.

The impact on me of immersing with Jane in her psychotherapy, and in her writing project, has also been notable. The connection I felt with her and my appreciation of her art led to my own transformative experience of immersion. I found my own strength and creativity to begin this book. These ideas have been swimming around in my mind for many years, yet I was lacking the immersive impetus to finally begin putting form to them. The mutuality of the immersive experience led both of us to risk beyond our safe zones.

Jane's experiences while writing her book illustrate how the creative process becomes one of entry-disengagement-reentry. It also points out the significant role that relationships with others play in that process. In part 2 we will take a closer look at the types of relationships that are needed for an artist to sustain creativity. But first let's explore a little more closely the process of moving in and out of immersive states.

IMMERSION, DISENGAGEMENT, REENTRY

In chapter 1, I described how the creative process involves a state of immersion (where the artist feels whole, complete, and cohesive), followed by a state of disengagement (where the artistic product is judged, evaluated, and tweaked). An artist will naturally flow between these states. When immersed, the artist is connected with the art form, and in this connection a transformation occurs both in the art and in the artist. When the artist disengages from the work, she is left with a new self, one that has been affected by the experience of immersion. Disengagement can be a quiet time of reflection, contemplation, and consolidation of the experience of immersion. When stepping back, the artist can feel strengthened and enhanced by the creative experience.

But the artist can also feel insecure, vulnerable, and full of self-doubt in this space of disengagement. Degas, for instance, once said to his fellow artist Max Liebermann, "I would like to be rich enough to buy back all my paintings and destroy them by pushing my foot through the canvas." The artist's openness and exposure during immersion can leave him feeling naked and at risk of humiliation. Psychological defenses come rushing in for protection. The artist is in desperate need of supportive responses from others, and here a healthy person can reach out for this support. I know myself that when I feel exposed and naked in the realm of writing, I turn to others to feel special, safe, and understood. Connections with others can provide me the strength to risk myself once again in writing.

In fact, it was at this point in my own project that I faced reentering immersion after a difficult disengagement. It was all the more frustrating because I was enjoying a fairly smooth immersive period and had cleared out time in my work schedule so I could continue to write — then I got blocked-scared-stuck. It wasn't a total waste, because I did get a lot of spring yard work done. (Our yard has never looked so good.) In this state, I did everything *but* write.

Here's what happened: I wrote through the first chapter and felt pretty pleased with the project so far. About that time, I saw in the newspaper that a musician I admire was playing in a smallish venue in town. Excited by the chance to see him perform, I got tickets. I had a hopeful fantasy that he would be interested in my book and that he might even be willing to offer his thoughts and feedback. I brought a copy of what I had written to the show with me, having learned that the musician is generous in giving autographs after a performance. After the show, I did get to meet him, and I gave him my chapter. He graciously accepted it, promising to read it as soon as he had time. I was excited with anticipation, imagining he would contact me with enthusiasm and support.

However, I couldn't get back to writing. My work was "out there." I began to feel stupid. He probably wouldn't read it or, if he did, probably wouldn't consider it worthy of response. I began to fear shame, embarrassment, and humiliation for proudly presenting it to him. I began to doubt the entire project. I lapsed into a mild depression. The enthusiasm and immersion that had felt so energizing and sustaining were now cast with doubt and fear. Where would I go from here? Would I give up on the project? But then what?

I called my father and found energy in this connection. He, too, is writing a book and also struggling to sustain immersion. "Writing is so hard!" he validated. We were twins in this way, which was quite comforting (especially since he is so accomplished). Also, he expressed admiration for my ideas and efforts. He affirmed that I did have something valuable to say and that he was looking forward to my next chapter. I could feel my strength and energy to reengage in the project slowly regenerate. This single interaction with my father was powerfully helpful to me because it incorporated all three kinds of relational experiences that propel people forward: mirroring, idealization (or hero), and twinship. In part 2 of this book, I will devote an entire chapter to describing each one of these types of relations. For now, I will simply note that I experienced mirroring from him (he affirmed that I had something of value to say), idealization (I admire him and hope to make him proud of me), and twinship (he is a fellow author and knew firsthand about the uncomfortable feeling of exposure and self-doubt).

Immersing into other realms was also helpful. I put on my favorite music that morning. Once again, listening to it vitalized me, and I did some dancing. I was able to immerse in dancing (despite my failing knees) and began to feel capable of reentering the writing space.

I sat down at the computer with the goal of immersing into the topic. My aim was to immerse for the sake of immersing and not with the expectation that I would write "the mother of all chapters." The first draft of this section was the result of that effort and, if nothing else, I was reengaged in the process.

Moving in and out of creative immersion is a process that cannot be avoided, but we can learn to trust that the process will move us along in our growth as artists and as people. What happens, though, when we disengage from creativity and have nowhere else to turn for alternative sources of strength? We get stuck with feelings of fear and vulnerability that can lead to a variety of psychological troubles. Many artists suffer periods of darkness and turmoil when they cannot be artistically productive. Perhaps this is because, by nature, artists tend to be sensitive and to feel things more deeply than the average person. Perhaps this psychological makeup is necessary to create art. This sensitivity contributes to their art as much as it may torture them. But I believe that artists are also vulnerable to a certain kind of darkness when they disengage from their work and have nowhere else to turn.

DARKNESS

Immersive experiences keep us vitalized, hopeful, and creative. However, for the myriad of reasons I describe in this book, allowing immersion is not always easy. Many of our fears and dreads keep us from being able to risk immersion. Also, for different people, different realms may be easier to immerse in than others. One person may be able to risk immersion in artistic endeavors but may not be as able to risk it in relationships. Another person may be readily able to immerse in athletics or spirituality but dread the experience in playfulness. People are confronted with their vulnerabilities in different ways and in different realms, which can lead to blocks in immersive capacity in those areas.

The darkness sets in when an artist disengages from his work and has nowhere else to immerse. It is a black space, void of the hope and energy that had previously propelled his creativity. It is a scary place, filled with ghosts and shadows of the past that threaten to reemerge. It is the place that artists fear but is, unfortunately, a place many know well.

Let me distinguish the darkness from pain. Being in pain does not mean being in the darkness. When an artist is in pain due to loss or grief, he does not necessarily feel a lack of hope. In fact, many artists create some of their most powerful work out of their pain. Despite their suffering, they retain the hope that if they express their pain in artistic form, it will be seen and understood by others. This hope to have their pain recognized and understood sustains their ability to immerse in creativity.

But the darkness holds no such hope. Here, the artist is alone and lost. The immersion she had previously experienced in her artwork is gone. And when there is not another safe place she can go for strength and comfort, she is left with hopelessness and despair. The darkness can be a momentary, fleeting experience or it can linger for long periods. Some artists then become severely depressed. Others will turn to addictions. Creativity dies in the dark.

Virginia Woolf for example, became depressed every time she finished writing a new book. Outside of creative immersion, she was extremely sensitive to what critics wrote about her work and experienced multiple depressions, which eventually led to her suicide. And Willem de Kooning, the very influential abstract expressionist painter, said, "Sure, sometimes I go through periods of real despair, look at my picture and say to myself, 'What the hell am I doing?' But to go back to scratch—what scratch? As an artist I am what I am now."

In the dark, the artist retreats. His withdrawal makes the possibility of connection with others even less likely. Paralyzed by his own fears, he is unable to trust others and unable to trust himself. He may feel anxious and restless — he knows he needs something but is unable to define it or reach for it. He has no direction, no purpose, no meaning. In this dark space, the artist can feel emotionally numb. With the absence of the vitalizing effects of immersion, everything feels flat and empty.

If you are in the darkness, what is the way out? Connection. Someone needs to know where you are. Someone needs to sit in the dark with you, understanding the blackness and accepting the darkness. It is from that connection, from feeling understood and less alone, that you will find a spark of light. But you must let someone know that you are in the dark.

Depression

The clinical definition of depression includes the inability to enjoy activities that were once enjoyable. Enjoyment is a large component of immersion. But I have witnessed depressed people who cannot immerse with any aspect in life. They feel detached, numb, and withdrawn. Nothing excites them. There is a generalized lack of energy and vitality that leads to lethargy, oversleep (or insomnia), and diminished connectedness with loved ones, coworkers, and their professions. Despair that they will never feel any differently begins to creep in.

It has been determined that some forms of depression are genetically inherited — or, I should say, that the *vulnerability* for depression is inherited. Usually it takes some life stressor to trigger a depressive episode. It is rather like the chicken-and-the-egg problem: does an inherited depression wipe out the capacity for immersion, or does a lack of immersive experience cause the depression? This is difficult to sort out, but in my clinical work I have definitely seen it occur both ways. Regardless of the onset, clinical treatment of the depression is important. Psychotherapy and often antidepressant medication are indicated.

Psychotherapy itself can be an opportunity for immersive experience. However, for some people, especially those who are depressed, it can take a long time to develop the level of trust with the therapist that is necessary to allow an interpersonal immersive experience. The empathic and understanding therapist can engage with the person at whatever level the client is able to connect on. In many instances, the hopeful promise of a future immersive relationship can strengthen the person to the point of generating some energy and vitality.

It is often helpful to clarify in what realms you had previously been able to immerse (spirituality, intimacy, art) and where there may be lingering attempts to experience immersion. I have two patients, unrelated, who were severely depressed. One is a writer and the other a graphic designer. Both had isolated themselves from others and had no significant relationship. Both were also blocked from immersing in their work. Interestingly, when discussing immersive realms, they both described the same immersive effort: both experienced their home as immersive, and both put effort into getting furniture that was deep and "holding." Even though alone and feeling "outside of life," both found comfort in their homes. I felt hopeful. It was a start. An immersive place to grow from. Of course, treatment entailed a much more complex understanding of how their histories and recent experiences had blocked their immersive capacities. But we were able to use home as an immersive place to start from.

Anxiety

A lack of immersion can also result in feelings of anxiety and restlessness. When there is a lack of immersive experience, life tends to lose its sense of meaning and purpose. This can lead to a profound sense of restlessness: the need for something indefinable and the inability to feel a sense of gratification. A lack of immersion can leave a person feeling lost and without direction.

Anxiety and its frequent companion panic are usually the result of feeling helpless or powerless. They can be experienced if a person is unaware of the need for immersion and looks in all the wrong places to try to soothe the anxiety. They can also be experienced if a person is well aware of the need to immerse but feels paralyzed by fear and dread. It is a painful experience to long for immersion (say, with another person) but to feel trapped and paralyzed in the fear that inhibits it.

Distrust

Distrust and paranoia are both blocks to immersion and the outcome of its absence. It takes a great deal of trust, in others and in the self, to risk immersion. If there is fundamental distrust, as in paranoia, a person will be unable to allow immersive experiences, especially in the interpersonal realm. It is interesting that such people will often create immersive spaces within their own thinking. They can immerse into the idea of distrust and often weave complex (and creative!) explanations about an unsafe world around them.

Underachievement

Underachievement is another symptom resulting from a lack of immersion. The underachiever cannot risk failure. It becomes safer not to immerse, not to try, lest one try and fail. It can also be a reflection of a lack of appreciation for the immersive experience itself. Often, underachievers come from homes where achievement and success are overvalued. The goal or end product is all that matters, and the process is not enjoyed or appreciated. Such a person's sense of specialness and fear of disappointing others are on the line every time he or she engages in a project. The price is too high, the competition too stiff. The solution is to withdraw from the race, but in the meantime, the person never learns to experience the joy of the process — the fulfillment of immersion itself.

Numbness and Isolation

Emotional numbness and social isolation are also symptoms of a lack of immersive experience. Here again, when the vitalizing effects of immersion are not present, everything feels flat and "on the surface." Connections with others feel meaningless. Social relatedness can begin to feel more like a burden, a drain of energy, rather than an energizing experience. People tend to retreat from others when this occurs because the payoff is not there. In this case, a person feels an "empty depression," not seriously sad or despairing, but flat and empty.

Anger

Aggression and violence can also result from a lack of immersive experience. Experiencing immersion is a natural, inborn need. When the family environment fails to provide and allow for immersion, the child is psychologically malnourished. Such children tend to grow up either depressed and detached or angry and defiant. Many turn to their peer groups for the experience of immersion, but a connection with other detached and angry peers can often lead to aggressive behavior. Some of the anger can be understood as legitimate resentment about not getting the needed support. But also, because of a lack of immersive experience, the selves of these children are typically undeveloped and quite fragile. Such people have not been able to develop a solid sense of self-esteem and respect for others. Any perceived insults to their fragile sense of self can lead to anger and rage. Rage is a by-product of a threatened self, and many angry youth do not have much resilience to bounce back from the bumps and bruises we all sustain in our psychological life. These kids are desperately in need of immersive experience with others. And many have not experienced immersion in any other realm than perhaps with their peer groups and with drugs and alcohol.

ADDICTIONS

In the dark, some artists turn to drugs, alcohol, casual sex, gambling, food, or other behaviors to feel better, because these activities can provide a temporary experience of immersion. People turn to substances or other behaviors (such as gambling, TV watching, workaholism) to help them feel relaxed and soothed or strengthened and vitalized. Some psychoactive drugs (such as cocaine, marijuana, LSD) can even initially increase the user's capacity to immerse in other realms. Because these drugs lower inhibitions and psychological defenses, states of immersion are more easily experienced. The user may have a flurry of new ideas, a new appreciation of sound, color, or touch, and a profound sense of spiritual connectedness. These states of immersion are the high, and they are what the user hopes to experience again and again. However, this increased capacity for immersion through drugs, alcohol, or other activities is usually temporary and short-lived. Addictions can develop as the user continues to seek these immersive states, especially if ever larger doses are needed.

In this way, I understand the use of drugs, alcohol, and other behaviors as pseudo-immersive experiences: they temporarily fill a person's need for immersion but do not generate creativity and hope. In fact, rather than strengthening the person, these compensatory efforts for a lack of immersion or interpersonal connection leave him feeling even more despairing and lost. These behaviors are like a blanket that covers up and numbs the darkness but does not take it away.

People turn to taking drugs and other compulsive behaviors when they have given up on others to provide the emotional support they need. Such disappointments often begin early in childhood. The child who is consistently given a pacifier or blanket instead of being picked up and held learns to turn to inanimate objects for comfort and soothing. The child who is forced to cry himself to sleep out of the parents' fear that he will become overly dependent if they soothe him will learn to stop asking for support and will stop anticipating interpersonal immersion. I am not saying that a parent can never frustrate a child's needs. I am referring to "average expectable experience." When the parent *more often than not* responds to a child's needs for connection, this child continues to trust that others are available and trustworthy providers of support. Paradoxically, this experience of being securely connected with others facilitates our individual capacities to self-soothe and to bounce back from injuries or disappointments. We become more resilient, self-confident, and independent when we are used to being solidly connected. In contrast, the child who is continually and even systematically frustrated ("so he'll learn to do it for himself") will learn that other people are not a reliable source of comfort and will instead turn to other means to self-calm and self-soothe.

Another powerful dimension of these pseudo-immersive activities is that they are often engaged in within the context of a social group. The dynamics of the social group often provide the individual with much-needed connection with others. These relationships can provide sustaining, immersive benefits to their members. For example, within cults and gangs, and even among drinking buddies, members can find a sense of belonging, whereas before they had felt isolated and alone. Also, there is often a leader within the group whom members respect and admire. Special status based on drinking ability or fighting skill can elevate individual members' self-esteem. Thus, members of the group can feel safe and special and that they belong somewhere. The group can be a powerful, sustaining psychological force for its members, making the activity even that much harder to give up. It would mean giving up a strong identity and connection with others, which is lacking in many addicts' isolated and alienated lives.

All of these considerations point to the importance of a new peer group when rehabilitating from an addiction. One way of building a new peer group is through a 12-step program. The philosophy behind the 12-step programs, such as Alcoholics Anonymous, is that the addict must both immerse with a higher power and turn to a sponsor within the group or to the group as a whole when he needs strength and support. With these new connections, the person can generate hope and the creativity needed to form a new life and new attachments.

LONGING FOR HOPE

I have mentioned the kinds of relationships that can pull you from the dark. If you do not have someone in your life who can be there with you, however, go to a therapist. Keep looking until you find a therapist who can understand and tolerate the darkness. (Some therapists are also afraid of the dark and will not be able to sit there with you.) You will know when you find a good fit with a therapist. You will feel that such a person is trying to understand and respect your experience. You will sense that he or she has the strength to sit in the dark for as long as it takes; this will give you hope to connect with the therapist and hope to immerse again.

The following is the story of a painter who lived a tragic life in desperate search of alternative immersive experiences. Because relationships had been so unsafe in his life, he turned to drugs, alcohol, and promiscuous sex and became severely depressed. His ability to resume painting was directly related to the hope he found in new connections with others.

Dan was thirty-five years old and single and held a leadership position in a local business. He explained that he was quite socially isolated despite being a successful and eloquent spokesman for his company. He felt depressed, angry, and detached from others. He revealed that he used drugs and drank alcohol in an effort to make himself feel better and to reduce his social inhibitions. Additionally, he had recently begun to seek out prostitutes. He felt ashamed of his behavior and feared that he would not be able to stop. He was aware that his connections with prostitutes served a strong psychological function. Sometimes he would not even have sex with them; he was mainly seeking companionship and holding. It was the only time in his desolate experience that he could feel connected to and immersed with another person. He was sad and angry that he felt he had to pay someone for this experience.

Dan had suffered a painful childhood. He was born to a single mother who had to work two jobs to make ends meet at home. Dan remembered being alone and on his own from a very early age. He recalled developing a streetwise tough-guy image to survive, and this facade thinly masked his internal world of fear and aloneness. His starvation for a protective figure led him to seek out companionship with several shady older boys. These disturbed young men sexually molested him when he was a young adolescent and beat him up on several occasions. Dan learned to be distrustful of others and survived on fantasies that he needed no one and could take care of himself.

Despite his painful psychological and physical existence, he was quite bright and found refuge in reading and sketching. He fantasized about becoming a famous journalist or artist. He imagined that through fame and fortune he would finally be seen, recognized, and appreciated. This fantasy provided him with the fuel for his academic and artistic efforts. In addition, he found a teacher who recognized his talents and supported him.

He pushed himself through high school and later college, earning strong marks for both his writing and his critical thinking. Although he was able to succeed academically, his internal life was organized around his view of the world as an unsafe and dangerous place and around his self-protective shell of fear and distrust of people. He coped by creating an alternate persona for himself. He described the adaptive, intelligent side of his personality as "Chip" and the broken, angry, depressed part as "the evil twin, Skip."

A thoughtful and intelligent man, Dan proceeded to give me an account of his many years of depression. He had obviously seen many therapists throughout his adult life and was psychologically minded in his reflections about his previous treatments. He had attempted suicide in his early twenties, which led to a psychiatric hospitalization. This hospitalization had been a traumatic experience for him: he did not feel that the staff made an effort to understand him. Instead, he was heavily medicated and was sent to do basket-weaving. During this hospitalization, he felt very alone and labeled.

There was, however, a nurse in his ward who showed him compassion and who listened to him. He sexualized this relationship in his mind and began to flirt with her. At the time, he was thrilled when she reciprocated his sexual innuendos and eventually had sex with him. Because sexual relations between patients and staff are strictly prohibited, they met secretly for their encounters.

The connection he felt with the nurse was very sustaining for him. He felt very special that she had chosen him. In fact, he described feeling strengthened by their relationship and began to feel some hope for his future. He dreamed of continuing their relationship publicly once he was released. She would provide him the loving connection he so desperately lacked in his life.

Dan began drawing again. Although he was not consciously aware of it at the time, in our therapy sessions he could reflect that his relationship with the nurse had given him the hope that if he expressed himself through drawing, his pain would be seen and understood. Also, she became someone he wanted to impress with his artistic talent.

However, the nurse suddenly rejected him. She had become frightened of discovery and abruptly ended all contact with him. He was devastated. He stopped drawing and retreated back into his isolation from others, once again convinced that people were not available to him or reliable sources of support.

It was years later when Dan came to me for therapy. He was understandably hesitant about trusting me: why wouldn't I, like all the other people in his life, eventually abandon and hurt him? I appreciated the risk he was taking in reaching out for my help, and instead of trying to reassure him that I was not like the others, I said that it made sense to me that he would be wary of trusting me. We would need to respect his dread to repeat the patterns from his past, while also appreciating his strength to reach out for a new kind of connection with me.

Our relationship involved moving back and forth on this continuum of dread and hope and, as he felt increasingly understood by me, he began to paint again. He said he had so much he needed to express through his painting, so much pain and anger and hurt, but that he had given up on being seen and understood. The paintings he produced were quite good; they were also dark and scary. Many were filled with violent, angry images. Dan described his work as reflections of his inner pain and angst. He had great talent with colors and shapes and was able to effectively convey the nature of his inner life. Even more than that, the paintings grabbed you, pulling you into his disturbing state of unrest and despair.

Dan held several shows where he displayed his collection. These shows were very gratifying for him because he witnessed the effect his work had on others. He told me that his mission in painting had been fulfilled: he had hoped to connect with others in such a way that they could see, feel, understand, and appreciate his pain. Of course, he was strengthened through praise he received for his talent and expressiveness. But the most profound impact for him was in feeling understood by his audience. The hope for this healing experience had been generated in his immersion in psychotherapy, and later in the painting. He told me this hope had been his incentive all along: he didn't fantasize about fame and fortune any longer (although he still thought they would be nice); he fantasized about *finally* being understood and connected with others. His painting had become his medium for undoing the aloneness he had felt since childhood.

THE LIGHT

The allure of immersion is the hope for a new beginning. We are all groping toward self-healing; we try to extract from others and from art what has been missing in our lives. In most cases, we know what we need: to feel special, to feel safe, to feel understood, and to feel connection. We all go about our business, alternating our efforts at getting these responses from others with retreating into our safe space for self-preservation. The hope in immersion is that we will finally receive (or sustain, if we've been lucky) the responses we need from others to feel strong and secure in the world.

The promise of immersion is that we will be reanimated and brought to life. We hope to experience ourselves in relation to others in a new way. We hope to feel "good enough," to be seen, recognized, validated, and valued. We hope to make our parents (or other significant parental figures) proud of us. We hope to feel respected among our peers. And we hope to be able to provide something meaningful to our own children and to others.

Each moment of standing at water's edge is charged with the energy of these hopes. We feel that we are standing at the forward edge of ourselves: contemplating taking the dive into creativity is vitalizing, strengthening, and energizing. We are on the brink of creating something new and reaching for something beyond what we know. The allure of immersion is that it will take us someplace that we've never quite been before — and what a blissful place that will be! Let us turn now in part 2 to the specific kinds of relationships with others that will either enable or inhibit our ability to dive into creativity.

GUIDES

I. BE AWARE OF AND RESPECT THE FEARS YOU ARE FACING.

Understand blocks as reasonable efforts at self-preservation. Don't interpret a block as evidence of your laziness, inadequacy, or unconscious wish for failure. Not only is this unhelpful; it is most likely untrue. Instead, take a deeper look at what fears you are facing. Is it a fear of inadequacy? A fear of your emotions? A fear of emptiness or having nothing to offer? A fear of annihilation of your identity or self-esteem? A fear of rejection? A fear of success? A fear of uncertainty and the unknown? A fear of exposure and humiliation?

Awareness of the fears that are blocking you is the first step in stretching beyond them. It is important to understand that these fears are not evidence of weakness. They are understandable and valid responses to previous experience. At one time, these fears helped you to adapt to and survive certain situations. Fears do not generally go away on their own. New experiences must convince you that it is now safe.

2. UNDERSTAND YOUR DREAD TO REPEAT.

When we are hurt, disappointed, or humiliated, we "dread to repeat" that injury again and will avoid re-creation of the experience. This is a natural human response, but although it helps to keep us safe, it also tends to inhibit our freedom to immerse. Luckily, we also tend to hold the hope for a new beginning, which can propel our efforts to try again.

Take a careful inventory of your previous experiences of disappointment, failure, or other injury. Try to identify specific moments of humiliation or failure. These are likely the roots of your dread to repeat. How did you cope with these injuries? Did you withdraw completely from the activity (creating, loving, or learning)? Did you generalize the injury you felt to other activities or to other parts of yourself? Or did you continue the activity but block yourself from immersing in it?

Now consider specific memories of success. It can be helpful to consciously explore these experiences of gratification. Write them down. These experiences likely fueled your trust in others and in yourself. These were experiences where immersion was safe. These experiences gave you hope for your future, for your capacity to express yourself and to be understood.

These concrete memories of injury and of success all contribute to your current constellation of fears, dreads, and hopes. Have empathy for that person who has survived, who has done the best he can, and who is struggling to balance the dread to repeat with the hope for a new beginning.

3. REACH OUT FOR SUPPORT.

When you disengage from creativity, turn to other relationships or activities to experience immersion. This will strengthen and comfort you so you can reengage in creativity. If you do not have alternative immersive realms to turn to, you may enter the dark. If you find that you are paralyzed, depressed, and isolated, see a therapist. A therapist can walk with you through your experience, helping you to understand the nature of your blocks as well as what you may need to resume forward movement. Everything is easier if you are not alone.

The most healing aspect of psychotherapy may well be that it provides immersive potential. When a safe relationship is created between therapist and patient, it can serve as an immersive experience in addition to providing a significant source of interpersonal support. However, the success of any psychotherapy depends on the goodness of fit between the therapist and patient. Do not feel trapped with a therapist if you do not feel this immersive potential. It is totally reasonable to expect a feeling of safety and connection. In fact, it is necessary for a successful outcome. You may need to try several therapists until you find one with whom you feel safe, special, and understood.

PART TWO

Relationships

Neither a lofty degree of intelligence nor imagination
nor both together go to the making of genius.
Love, love, love, that is the soul of genius.

— WOLFGANG AMADEUS MOZART

CHAPTER THREE

The Need for Others

For not only young children . . . but human beings of all ages are found to be at their happiest and to be able to deploy their talents to best advantage when they are confident that, standing behind them, there are one or more trusted persons who will come to their aid should difficulties arise. The person trusted provides a secure base from which his (or her) companion can operate. And the more trustworthy the base the more it is taken for granted; and the more it is taken for granted, unfortunately, the more likely is its importance to be overlooked and forgotten.

— J. BOWLBY, MD,
SEPARATION: ANXIETY AND ANGER

To begin my discussion about the importance of others in supporting the creative process, I would like to present an interview I had with Loren Long, an accomplished artist who has illustrated many books, including *Mr. Peabody's Apples* by Madonna, *I Dream of Trains* by Angela Johnson, a 2004 edition of *When I Heard the Learn'd Astronomer* by Walt Whitman, and the 2006 redo of the classic *The Little Engine That Could* by Watty Piper.

I met with Loren at a very comfortable and homey small coffeehouse. He seemed right at home there, casual and easygoing. "Everyone thinks that I am so laid-back and relaxed. But my wife will tell you that I am actually quite intense when it comes to my work."

I told Loren that I wanted to get a feel for his internal experiences as he works on a project. Specifically, I said, I was interested in the role of other people in his process. He quickly said that his wife is his biggest support. "She's not an artist, but she has great taste. I run everything by her, sometimes daily as I'm working on a project. She is my first level of screening. If she likes it, then I feel the confidence to proceed.

"My publishers' opinions are also very important to me," he continued. "Not just because they determine if my work is adequate. I admire and respect them a lot. I want them to like what I've done. I guess that, in general, I always need someone to like my work. If they don't, my self-doubts come to the surface. You know, like I'm not living up to the grand fantasies I have about myself or about what my work should look like. Although I generally have a pretty good sense about the quality of my work, if the publishers don't like it, sometimes I feel like I have been found out. Like the show is over; others have finally realized that I am not so good.

"I need ongoing feedback of all my work. Sometimes I need to protect it until I get it to a certain point — a point good enough for show — even for my wife."

Loren made a point of describing the decision he made years ago to keep his life and time balanced between his work and his family. "My wife and children are very important to me. I have artist friends who either are single or devote all of their time to their art and miss out on good relationships with their families. They are much more productive than me — more prolific — they put out a lot of work. But I didn't want to be an absent husband or father. My dad was always there for me — that's how I was raised. I am careful to prioritize time with my wife and kids. They make me feel good and they keep me grounded. Like when I got the deal to do the Madonna illustrations. It is hard to get too carried away with yourself as a big-time artist when you're picking up dog poop in the backyard. I dream about being the greatest. It gives me motivation to keep on swinging, but I keep myself in check by living a normal lifestyle. I remind myself that I am a working artist — like a blue-collar artist —and that keeps me grounded and more able to handle the frustrations that come up.

"I don't get paralyzed in drawing but I certainly have highs and lows throughout the process.

"I suppose that I have sacrificed my career somewhat by choosing to prioritize my wife and kids. Maybe I would produce more art if I isolated myself into my work."

"Loren," I said, "maybe you have chosen to prioritize your family because you have the strength to connect with them as well as with your art. Some artists seclude themselves in their studios because they are *unable* to immerse in relationships. They are too frightened of intimacy. I view your lifestyle as a sign of your strength, and I believe that your relationships with your wife and children support and enrich your ongoing capacity to create."

We all need relationships with others to be at our best. When we are surrounded with support, we are more productive, happy, and energetic. Positive relationships help to move us forward and help us to grow. Positive relationships also help the artist along in his creative process. Good relationships can bolster our courage to take the plunge into creativity. And likewise, not-so-good relationships, or a lack of relationships, can inhibit our dive. What kinds of relationships do you need to sustain your creativity? And how do you develop these kinds of relationships? This section will address this dimension of the creative process, which has been woefully ignored.

Although most people will agree that relationships are an important part of their life and that relationships help them to feel strong and capable, many people have a difficult time developing and sustaining these supports. In fact, many, many people I see for psychotherapy live with the illusion of self-sufficiency. Our Western culture has placed so much emphasis and value on independence and autonomy that many people feel ashamed and weak when they are not able to handle everything by themselves. "I should be able to do it by myself," "I shouldn't be so reliant on others for my self-esteem," and "I should be able to help myself" are typical statements by the majority of people I see in my office (and that I know personally!). The epidemic of self-sufficiency is so widespread that it has infiltrated our marriages, our schools, our friendships, and our psyches. Not all cultures share this perspective. In Japan, the concept of the self-with-other is at the opposite extreme. In that culture, independence and individuality are viewed as negative traits. Japanese culture, instead, views connection and belonging to the group (family, marriage, collective society) as the highest state of being.

I believe that we are at our best when we find a middle ground between these two extremes of independence and dependence. Mutual relationships, where we respond to the needs of the other while maintaining our own sense of self, are optimal. In addition, relationships are the fertile ground in which our uniqueness and strength grow. From this perspective, we can begin to appreciate how relationships with others are a critical part of initiating and sustaining the creative process.

I have described how relationships with others are an important alternative realm of immersive experience that we can turn to for strength and rejuvenation when we disengage from creativity. But I will go even further to argue that our creative activity is undertaken in the first place in the hopes of generating certain kinds of relationships. Therefore, I believe that our experience of self-in-connection-with-others is so vital that it lies at the heart of most of what we do.

Before I delve deeper into this seemingly radical point of view, let me offer a brief summary of the movement in psychological theory toward this conclusion.

REVOLUTIONS IN DEPTH PSYCHOLOGY

In the past twenty years, new ways of understanding human behavior have revolutionized depth, or insight-oriented, psychological thinking. Contemporary psychoanalytic theories (such as self psychology, intersubjectivity theory, social constructivism, and others) and a growing body of research on infant and childhood development now challenge the very basic underlying assumptions behind older psychoanalytic approaches. These fascinating shifts in theory help us to understand our psychological experiences in a new way and point to the importance of our interpersonal relationships in feeling and being at our best.

The classical psychoanalytic model was based on Freudian concepts. Freud concluded that infants were "merged" with their mothers at birth, that newborns could not distinguish themselves as separate from their mothers and had no independent identity of their own. The child's developmental task throughout life was to become separated and independent from the mother. Freud then understood adult anxieties and fears as problems with this separation process.

Freud also believed that humans have innate, primitive drives for aggression and sex. Becoming a mature and healthy person meant being able to channel, or sublimate, these primitive drives (the *id* part of the personality) into rational and productive activities. Creativity was one such activity, and creative immersion was viewed as a relatively healthy way to sublimate these primitive urges rather than to act on them. For Freud, rational thought (the *ego* part of the personality) was the hallmark of mental health. Classical psychoanalysis thus viewed psychological development and growth as consisting of becoming increasingly independent of others and translating primitive urges for sex and aggression into something socially acceptable and rational.

However, around the same time, a different perspective was being developed about the nature of psychological health and development. D. W. Winnicott (1886–1971), a British psychoanalyst, proposed that a person matures and develops through connections with others. He believed that a child's dependence on the mother actually helped him gain his own independence. The child could develop and mature only within relationships with others. In contrast to Freud, with his ideas about creativity stemming from the socially undesirable id part of the personality, Winnicott viewed creativity as coming from a "transitional space," a space of play and interaction with others, which was critical for "the child's finding and becoming a self.... It is ... an intermediate area of *experiencing* to which inner reality and external life both contribute and it exists as a resting place for the individual engaged in the perpetual task of keeping inner and outer reality separate yet inter-related."

Winnicott described the area of "potential space" in a way that closely resembles the idea of creative immersive experience:

> Potential space is infused with primitive creativity, which later extends to all cultural phenomena, such as the areas of play and artistic creativity and appreciation, and of religious feeling, and of dreaming, and also of fetishism, lying and stealing, the origin and loss of affectionate feeling, drug addiction, the talisman of obsessional rituals, etc.... Potential space is a special space, in which the true self shines brightly, reflected into an other's bright light.

A cross section of recent psychological theories of development shows a shift from independence to the capacity to attach with others as the central factor in mental health. For example, the psychoanalyst Michael Balint emphasized the importance of seeking out and enjoying "symbiotic experiences" in his book *The Basic Fault*: "The aim of all human striving is to establish — or probably re-establish — an all-embracing harmony with one's environment, to be able to love in peace." He observed that opportunities for merging are often denied in the early mother-child relationship, leading to psychological symptoms and distrust of others. Although he believed people could never really be cured of the impact of lack of secure attachments (the "basic fault"), he also argued that through merging moments of "harmonious oneness" that occur throughout life, people can become able to feel more content and whole. These moments of harmonious oneness were most common in interpersonal relationships, but they could also be found in religious experiences, in artistic creations, and even during certain phases of analytic treatment. He also noted, "These intense experiences can appear to the outside observer as states of . . . withdrawal, when, in fact, for the individual, they are states of intense connectedness."

Contemporary theories support Winnicott's ideas, as we are now coming to view the ability to attach with others as a central feature of healthy psychological functioning. The shift from viewing healthy development as separating from the mother to viewing it as attaching with others has had profound implications in the field of psychology. Recent research in child development and child-parent interactions has found that psychological growth actually occurs within the *context* of relationships and not apart from them. In this way, it has been found that the child's capacity to be alone actually develops not by being alone but by being in the mother's presence. How can this be so? We can make sense of this paradox by understanding the strengthening quality of immersion. The more the parent is "present with" and available to the child, responding to the child's needs for connection and holding (physical and emotional), the more powerful and confident the child becomes. In the interaction between parent and child, the child feels connected to and supported by a powerful other, which bolsters his own sense of competence. We can think of connection with others as the psychological nutrition we require to grow. And as with food, we take in the connection with others and it becomes a part of our self; the connection helps us to feel strong and capable as an individual. And even if we are fed a regular diet of empathy and connection and have grown in our strength and self-confidence, we continue to need to eat to function at our best. Similarly, we never stop needing connection with others.

As opposed to viewing infants as dependent, clinging, or weak, modern psychological models see them as independent, assertive, and strong. The infant is psychologically complete as long as she is understood and responded to by others. It is important to note again that this need for empathy and response from others does not end in infancy or childhood. It is not a phase of development that one grows out of; it is a lifelong need. Healthy psychological development consists of becoming more adept in connecting with others, both in eliciting the kinds of support we need and in providing it to others.

People are at their best psychologically, cognitively, and emotionally when they experience this mutual give-and-take. Although the important experience lies in the connection with another person, it does not mean that we must give up our individuality. Quite to the contrary, these moments of connection actually enhance our sense of uniqueness and self-confidence.

Daniel Stern, a prominent researcher in child development, describes the importance of the experience of *merger*: "Mergers are simply the actual experience of being with someone (a self-regulatory other) such that self-feelings are importantly changed. During the actual event, the core self is not breached [that is, the infant still views the other as 'separate']. . . . The self experience is indeed dependent upon the presence and action of the other, but it still belongs entirely to the self. There is no distortion [between self and other]."

Even the challenge of learning language can be viewed as evolving out of moments of immersion and connection. As parent and child play with sounds and words, a potential space develops between them. This beginning language, which at first consists of sounds only the parent understands, evolves out of shared experience and connection. Together, parent and child creatively mold joint understandings that eventually lead to words and sentences.

In summary, in classical (Freudian) theory, people were understood as motivated by drives for aggression and sex and were viewed as struggling to achieve separation and individuation from the parents. New theories and research now understand people as driven toward relationships (aggression is merely an outcome of feeling threatened or injured in relationships) and as struggling to cocreate attachments with others that fulfill basic psychological needs to feel special, safe, and understood. Whereas classical psychoanalysis defined a person's character and personality by the id, ego, and superego, contemporary psychoanalysis asserts that a person can be fully understood only within the context of his relationships. With one person we may feel strong, confident, and secure, and with another person we may feel weak, frightened, and fragile. Healthy development and functioning consist of becoming increasingly adept in eliciting the responses we need from others and, in turn, learning how to provide others with the responses they need.

These are major shifts in how we view ourselves and others and in how we view the challenge of growing up. Rather than striving to become self-sufficient and independent of others, we must seek to become better at creating gratifying relationships. In order to be a strong person, you do not need to do it all by yourself. In fact, you cannot be creative in a vacuum.

Recent popular literature on creativity has focused on identifying the traits or qualities of creative people that distinguish them from "non-creative people." This literature has explored the personality types of famous artists and has identified their lifelong tendencies for perseverance, individuality, and drive. Other studies have looked at

PET scans, or brain imaging pictures, of artists and people engaged in creativity. These pictures of the brain in action have distinguished certain parts of the brain that are used during creativity. Although very interesting in its scope, however, all of this research assumes that either individuals have the capacity for creativity or they don't, that either individuals have the personality type to be creative or they don't.

By contrast, I am arguing that the capacity to be creative is much more fluid and changing and that even prolific artists are not able to be creative all of the time. Creativity is more of a psychological state and process. Most certainly it requires persistence, resilience, and determination on the part of the artist, but these traits are not a static or given ability. The moment-to-moment, project-to-project capacity to be creative emerges when we feel psychologically strong, safe, and understood by others. The more support that you can reach out for, accept, and provide, the more you will be helped along in your creative process. However, we are not all blessed with perfectly supporting others. Before beginning our examination of the specific kinds of relationships that strengthen our capacity to immerse in creativity and how to go about making these kinds of relationships, let's look at how imagining connections with others can be a healthy substitute.

IMAGINING CONNECTION

We all need relationships that help us to feel special, safe, and understood. Real-life relationships that foster these feelings in us are the fundamental ground in which we find the courage and hope that we need to create. But what if we do not have such relationships in our life? Is creativity impossible?

Karen Walant, PhD, in *Creating the Capacity for Attachment*, points out that "mankind's natural orientation is to be immersed in relationships, whether they be in internal or external contact with others." In other words, we are inclined toward connection and can be strengthened even by imagining these kinds of support. In the absence of real-life supportive relationships (or in addition to the ones we might already enjoy), the healthy, forward-moving part of our self reaches for this experience of connection through imagination. We fantasize about an appreciative audience or pleasing someone we admire and respect or belonging to a group of peers who understand and appreciate our work. Imagining supportive connections provides us the fuel to continue our attempts at creative immersion and sustains us through the various blocks and fears we encounter along the way.

Let me give you an example. I have danced since I was an adolescent. Unlike many of my friends, I did not take dance classes when I was a little girl. Instead, I have always been a private dancer — no dance recitals or rehearsals or competition. I enjoyed dancing in the privacy of my bedroom, moving the furniture and twirling around it. I enjoyed making up dances and practicing them over and over. I never intended to perform for anyone. In fact, in my heart of hearts, I knew that I was not technically proficient and could not compete with more trained dancers. But the privacy of my dancing allowed me to immerse in it quite easily. Even though no one was watching — and I didn't want anyone to watch because then I would become self-conscious and insecure — I entertained a continuous fantasy of being onstage, in front of an audience. I imagined that the audience loved my dancing. I would elaborate the fantasy to include dancing alongside my favorite musical performers, being their dancer.

I used this fantasy (and still do) to sustain my creative immersion in dance. The fantasy pushes me to continue to try new moves, to practice old moves, and to choreograph new dances. I have never told anyone about these fantasies before. They are (were) my little secret, and I suppose I have felt embarrassed to admit that I fantasize about such things, especially because I have never trained to be a professional dancer. It is just my hobby, my enjoyment of immersing in movement. But these fantasies have been quite real to me over the years. I don't know what else would have sustained my immersion in dance if I had not fantasized about such things.

Actually, imagining connections with others can be the seeds of creative urge. If we can imagine having an impact, being understood, or making a difference, we are energized to action. We use fantasy to begin and sustain our creativity. An actor I worked with revealed his sustaining fantasy: "I imagine hearing the applause, feeling filled up by how brilliant they think I am." Another woman, now a renowned opera singer, described how "As a child, I used to play that I was the conductor of a huge orchestra and would imagine receiving standing ovations. Who am I kidding? I still have that fantasy." And a writer said, "I suppose that down deep I believe that my book will change the world. I will be famous. I will be rich. I will be respected."

The types of connections we imagine (often subconsciously but almost constantly in our moment-to-moment experience) have a powerful impact on our capacity to enter into an immersive state. When we pay attention to this dimension of our internal experience, we realize how our capacity to immerse is determined by the nature of our imagined connections. If we imagine being seen, heard, and understood by others, we are more likely to risk creative immersion. In the absence of actual relationship connections, the healthy parts of our selves reach for them through imagination.

Many artists I've worked with are, in actuality, socially isolated or withdrawn but have healthy inner strivings about connecting with others through their art. The stereotype of the socially alienated artist may often hold true in real life, but internally they are able to experience connection with others through artistic expression. Some of them have been silenced in previous interpersonal relationships but, instead of completely losing hope of feeling understood, have been able to experience connection with others through their art form. These artists typically experience an easier flow into creative immersion because it has become the safest and most hopeful way of imagining and experiencing connection with others. Vincent van Gogh once said, "I want to touch people with my art. I want them to say 'he feels deeply,' 'he feels tenderly.'"

All along I have been saying that supportive relationships are critical to initiating and sustaining the creative process. What kinds of relationships do we need to facilitate our creativity? And what gets in the way of developing these kinds of relationships? The remaining chapters in this section will describe three important kinds of relationships that help to boost our courage so that we may immerse into creativity. Certain types of relationships actually strengthen our psychological core, which then helps us to take risks because we feel less fragile. Having a more solid psychological base gives us the feeling that we will be more resilient, more able to bounce back if we do get hurt along the way. We will need to turn to these kinds of relationships many, many times in the course of an artistic project. They will support us, be a refuge for us, and help us to get beyond the blocks of fear we will undoubtedly face in our journey. In fact, the types of relationships described here are fundamental experiences we all need in our everyday functioning. Having these kinds of relationships helps us to feel and be at our best in all areas of our life.

At the risk of splitting hairs, I want to make a couple of clarifications. The point in describing these relationships is to show that they provide us with an internal experience. It is actually the *internal* experience itself that we need — the relationship is the thing that creates and allows the internal experience to exist. These feelings are the pillars of the personality and eventually determine many of our behaviors, our hopes, and our fears. I will talk about the kinds of relationships that provide us with three internal fundamental experiences: feeling special, feeling safe, and feeling understood. In an ongoing way, we need mirrors to validate our sense of being special, heroes to help us feel safe, and twins to help us feel understood. The internal experiences of feeling mirrored, of admiring a hero, and of feeling like others can occur with the same person at different times or even all at once with one person.

CHAPTER FOUR

Finding Strength in Mirrors

Our deepest fear is not that we are inadequate. Our deepest fear is that we are powerful beyond measure. It is our light not our darkness that frightens us. We ask ourselves, who am I to be brilliant, gorgeous, talented and fabulous? Actually, who are you not to be?

— MARIANNE WILLIAMSON, *A RETURN TO LOVE*

The artist who feels special and great is likely to create. At the same time, artists create with the hope of being seen and recognized. These are healthy human strivings and are the basis for solid, resilient self-esteem.

Contemporary psychology theory postulates that the self is partly defined by feelings of grandiosity: it is the part of us that wants to be "looked at and admired." We need others to see our specialness and to reflect it back to us. I call these people who validate our strengths, our talents, and our uniqueness *mirrors*.

CHILDHOOD EXPERIENCE

Feeling special and unique helps facilitate an artist's entry into immersion. This feeling is often viewed as a negative thing: it implies arrogance, self-centeredness, and snobbishness. However, I am referring to this experience in a slightly different manner. Everyone has a need to feel valued, special, and recognized. It is the experience of having power and value. These feelings are the basis for self-esteem.

Many theorists believe that people are born with this feeling of specialness. Babies have this foundation of self-esteem as a mechanism for survival. Imagine the infant who cries because she is hungry and *fully expects* to be recognized and fed. The moment of connection between hungry infant and feeding mother validates this feeling. It is an immersive moment for both mother and infant. The mother's milk is the nutritional nourishment, and her recognition of the baby is the psychological nourishment. The baby and mother come out of this experience a little stronger (physically and psychologically) and better off. The baby has gotten her need for recognition met and can now move on to other experiences. If the baby is not responded to, everything else stops while the baby vigorously asserts her need to be seen and fed. Her attempts to be recognized, through crying and reaching movements, reflect her hope of a response and are healthy forward strivings toward connection and, ultimately, growth. If, however, she is repeatedly ignored or criticized for her assertive behavior, she may lose her hope for connection and simply give up and die. Silence is not always golden.

As a child grows, his sense of being special and great expands into feeling invincible. Now imagine the toddler who dresses up as his favorite superhero. In his play, he is not pretending to be the hero, he *is* the hero. The toddler believes he has unlimited power. (This is why parents must keep a constant eye on children of this age, because they often believe they *can* fly out of the window.) Perhaps children need this fantasy to counteract an underlying feeling of being small and helpless. The child's fantasy of power and greatness is validated when the parent reflects this back to the child and exclaims, "Here comes Superman!" The attuned parent knows not to challenge this fantasy by correcting the child's self-perception. By going along with the fantasy, parents help keep the rudiments of the child's self-esteem intact.

However, many well-intentioned parents feel they should try to protect their child from the ultimate disappointment of discovering he does not have superpowers by correcting his fantasy. "Johnny, you know that you can't really fly." In an effort to teach the child the limits of reality, such parents believe they are deflating the child's grandiose fantasies for his own good. However, the child may experience this kind of response as a deflation of his entire sense of himself and his strength. When a child's fantasies of greatness and specialness are shattered in this way, he may need to hold on to the fantasy even more tightly in an effort to preserve his sense of power, or he may begin to fear devastation to his self-esteem if he dares to have any dream of being somebody.

If the child's fantasy of being superhuman is allowed to remain intact, his feeling of being special and great will naturally moderate and become more realistic. When the child discovers that he cannot, in fact, fly, he will integrate this moment of reality into his identity but will not lose his fundamental sense of strength. These bumps and bruises to his inflated feeling of specialness will undoubtedly occur without his parents having to purposefully strip away his unrealistic self-perceptions. When this process occurs naturally and the parents are there, instead, to recognize and empathize with these humbling bouts with reality, the child's fundamental feeling of specialness will remain solid as the basis for a more realistic self-esteem and pride.

A painful example of disappointing a child's need for a reflection of her greatness comes to mind. A school-age child proudly displays to her mother a drawing she made at school. She is hopeful to see the gleam in her mother's eye, to see her accomplishment reflected in her mother's pride. "Look at my picture!" she exclaims. The mother, preoccupied with other things, fails to match the child's enthusiasm and responds with a distracted, "That's nice." Or, worse yet, the mother finds fault with some aspect of the picture, even though her intention is to help make it better. The child is deflated. Her voice and body language go limp, and her enthusiasm for her own work withers.

In this scenario, the mother failed to reflect, or mirror back, her daughter's feeling of greatness. And the price for the child was high. She had every expectation of being seen and affirmed by her mother — she was enthusiastic, open, and without defense. When her mother failed to affirm her, she felt humiliated for feeling so proud and also felt disappointed in her mother. Her sense of competency was injured. "Maybe I'm not a good painter" and "I won't show my mom my work anymore" are possible outcomes of this moment. She will likely be more hesitant and tentative when approaching her next painting, her disappointment in this moment having created an obstacle to immersion. She now has a brick of self-consciousness about her painting (which, if replicated, could begin to build a strong wall blocking her ability to immerse) and a self-protective shield about being enthusiastic about her own work.

The reverse of this scenario can also have detrimental effects on a child's sense of greatness and thus immersive capacity. Say a parent loudly applauds *anything* a child does or creates. If the child is not proud of a drawing, or doesn't put much effort into it, and a parent responds with too much enthusiasm, there is also no immersive connection. This child feels that the parent's enthusiasm is not an accurate reflection of him, either. He does not resonate with the applause. This child, too, steps outside of his internal experience and into observation and evaluation of himself or the parent. Often, the parent's applause then becomes meaningless in all endeavors, and the child's need for a reflection of his own unique sense of specialness goes unmet.

The need for a reflection of our sense of greatness does not end in childhood. This need for admiring others continues throughout life, and receiving it can sustain immersion. I think of my own experience when giving a talk or presentation. If I feel that the audience is receptive and appreciative of what I have to say, I am more able to immerse in my subject area and in the performance. Seeing, every so often, the appreciative nod of a kind face in the audience, or witnessing an audience member becoming energized and enthusiastic by the topic, helps me to be at my best. These reflections of my specialness, or my need to feel significant and of value, help me to immerse in the project at hand. Often I have found that I am able to become more creative in these moments. A new example may come to mind or a new way of conveying the material will occur to me. I am more apt to be spontaneous and playful and to feel an increased engagement with the audience when they think I am special and great. Thus, receiving appreciative feedback allows me to enter into immersive realms and typically enhances and deepens my performance.

On the other hand, if I sense the audience is bored, uninterested, or critical of what I am presenting, it is very difficult for me to find an immersive state. Internally, I begin to doubt the material and myself. I become self-conscious. I am suddenly an observer of myself and, at times, my own worst critic. Outside of the immersive state, my experience begins to resemble the phenomenon of tripping over your feet if you think about how to walk. Not only does my creativity become blocked, but even my cognitive and intellectual capacities become clouded. This sensitivity to an audience's reaction is not a sign of fundamental weakness or insecurity. It is part of the natural, mutual interplay between ourselves and others that constitutes our state of self at any moment. Even the most self-confident person needs to feel validated by others (whether that is a group of people or a single person) to be at his or her best and to keep going in an endeavor. If we perceive a negative reaction in others, we lose our sense of safety in play and in our freedom to immerse.

In an essay included in the book *Significant Others*, Louise De-Salvo describes the positive impact that a new, appreciative friend had on Virginia Woolf:

Though Virginia Woolf's work was well respected when she met her new friend, she never felt herself to be a success. Her Bloomsbury circle rarely praised her. Often, under the guise of honesty, they mocked and derided her so severely that she suffered anguish and feelings of self-hatred. Vita, instead, gave her the praise and respect that she both longed for and deserved.

FEELING SPECIAL AND THE CAPACITY TO IMMERSE

I have never talked with an artist who is able to sustain immersion over a long period of time without finding this reflection of his or her own greatness in someone. Most artists need to have someone who admires and appreciates their work in progress at many steps along the way. After an immersive period, the artist, who was previously oblivious to audience evaluation, needs to step out of the immersion to objectively assess the work. As I stated earlier, at this point in the process, the person may feel vulnerable and exposed. She may doubt her work and her talent and skills. She begins to fear that, perhaps, she is not so great. Often this fear extends beyond the work itself. Because she has invested her total self into the work, rejection and criticism can feel like a demolishment of her entire being. She is in need of a supportive, appreciative response from someone else so that she can return to the work and to another immersive state.

This is the point where childhood and lifelong history influence how we will deal with current blocks. If the artist's typical and average experience in the past was to be positively seen by others, then she will anticipate positive future support. This person expects and hopes to see the gleam in another's eyes and will reach out for support. Or this person can turn to her positive fantasies of a *perceived* audience. She can call up an imagined appreciative audience to bolster her fragile sense of being great and special, which will ultimately help her to reimmerse.

If, however, the person typically experienced critical or indifferent responses from others in the past, he will not tend to trust others to supply a positive mirror and may withdraw and become stuck in this space of disengagement. Unable to trust that others will be supportive, this person retreats and loses the forward edge of his hope and creativity. He may experience depression and anxiety and lose the strength to reengage with the project.

Recall the case of Jane in chapter 2. You may remember that her *perceived audience* was hostile. The abuse and criticism she had experienced from her father while growing up led her to anticipate a similarly hostile response from her current audience. Her feeling of being special and great, which had been restored through her previous successful book projects, had been supplanted by self-sabotage, fear, and the sense of being a fraud, issues she'd struggled with throughout her life. She needed to distinguish her past experience from her current one in order to take in and make use of the real positive reflections she was receiving from her publisher, her fans, and me.

CONSTRUCTIVE FEEDBACK AND CRITICISM

How, then, does an artist receive useful, constructive feedback from others in order to improve his work? Once a person has been adequately affirmed for his strengths and efforts, he is more ready to integrate alternative ideas. I know that I can tolerate corrections much more easily when I feel that the essence of what I have done is appreciated. If I do not feel that I have first been validated, I hear any constructive criticism as devaluing. When this happens, instead of feeling helped by the remarks, I lose energy for the project, and my sense of competency suffers. It is amazing what a difference it makes for me if criticisms or suggestions of my work are preceded by an acknowledgment of my brilliance.

The stereotype of the narcissistic, self-centered artist comes from this dimension of the immersive experience. By and large, people who were not adequately reflected throughout their lives need bigger and more frequent amounts of real applause to sustain their work. Of course, applause can be sought for its own sake, and not in the service of immersion. If a person does not use reflections of his greatness to further immersive activity, this kind of gratification moves the process out of a creative arena and into a more nonproductive or addictive realm. Perhaps Henri Matisse had the most stabilizing perspective when it came to receiving criticism, by viewing his artwork and its feedback as a method of communicating with others:

> I have always sought to be understood and, while I was taken to task by critics or colleagues, I thought they were right, assuming I had not been clear enough to be understood. This assumption allowed me to work my whole life without hatred and even without bitterness toward criticism, regardless of its source. I counted solely on the clarity of expression of my work to gain my ends.

BLOCKS AND FEARS

Just as relationships with others provide the support we need to feel special and great, they can also injure this perception of ourselves. Problems associated with our social supports (or, more accurately, with the feeling about ourselves in relation with others) can lead to blocks to immersion and creativity.

Very few (if any) of us have such a solid base of self-esteem that we would not be affected by negative, critical, or even indifferent feedback. We all continue to need affirmation from those around us. And since immersion requires a total investment of self, what is created out of the immersive space is deeply personal and revealing. In this exposed state, we are very sensitive to criticism or assault.

The following are common fears and blocks that artists face in the realm of feeling special and great. To truly understand and appreciate the fears you are facing, you must understand how these fears or blocks make sense in your own life, in your own life narrative. You may see how the block is actually functioning in the service of self-preservation, though at a cost to productivity and fulfillment.

Absence of Positive Mirroring in Childhood

We all need to feel recognized, seen, and appreciated. When someone important to us recognizes our talents and skills, our self-esteem and self-confidence are enhanced. If there is no one there to reflect us or if the only reflection we receive is critical or devaluing, it is very difficult to muster the strength and courage required to dive headfirst into immersion.

If you do not have appreciative others, then finding and developing those kinds of relationships will be an important overall part of your creative process. Often, we have people around us who do not seem to appreciate our work. Indeed, if you grew up without positive mirroring from others, then perhaps you do not expect to receive this kind of affirmation. You may have given up on receiving positive support, so you have probably quit even asking for it. Part of your task in facing the dive into creativity will consist of stretching beyond your assumptions and expectations of disappointment and asking clearly for what you need from those around you. More often than not, people are pleased to be supportive but often do not know how. Tell them what you need to hear. One writer would play the "Tell me" game with a colleague: "Tell me I can write"; "Tell me this story is good"; "Tell me I am not a fraud." Whenever she felt paralyzed by feelings of vulnerability and insecurity, she would call the other, and they would take turns asking for what they needed. Sounds silly, but it worked.

Don't underestimate the power of imaginary support. When support is missing in real life, try to imagine someone, or an entire audience, being appreciative of your work. For example, a sculptor described a fantasy relationship with her deceased mother. After her mother died, she was able to feel sustained by her belief that her mother was watching her from heaven and that her mother "would be so proud" of her work or would really *understand* her latest piece. In fact, their real-life relationship had had its ups and downs. She recalled that her mother had not been perfectly attuned to her work and her efforts when she was alive. But now that her mother was dead, she was actually able to imagine her mother as fully present and appreciative. She reasoned that her mother could now put her own worries aside (which had, before, gotten in the daughter's way of total focus on her sculpting). Now, she could imagine having her mother's total attention and recognition, and she has been very productive artistically since her mother's death.

Fear of Exposure and Not Being Good Enough

The fear of not being good enough blocks many of us from diving into immersive states. The anticipation of rejection or criticism can be a powerful barrier to allowing ourselves to let go and be swept along in creation. This fear of negative evaluation paralyzes our capacities to let go of our strong grip on the safe, the familiar. It is much safer to stay where we are; nothing risked, nothing lost. People will preserve themselves at almost any cost. And this is the problem when it comes to the capacity to immerse.

When immersing in a project or relationship, we are totally exposed. In a meaningful immersive experience, we lay bare our most vulnerable sensitivities and reveal the essence of our insides. Our entire self is on display. It is difficult to separate ourselves from our work. In this way, we feel that it is not merely the "product" that is evaluated. A rejection of the product is a rejection of ourselves.

A rejection or criticism in this state of exposure is experienced as an injury to our most primitive, fundamental feeling of greatness. Some people will never recover from such a hit. Many people will abandon any future attempts to immerse in that particular realm. They feel too vulnerable and too distrusting to risk such injury again. Consider the artist who is given a bad critique and never paints again, or the lover who is betrayed and never again gives his heart away.

The potential injury to self-esteem embedded in criticism or rejection is obviously substantial within an immersive experience. We can feel the risk of devastation is too great: we procrastinate or avoid immersion altogether. We assume a self-protective stance from the start, never fully investing ourselves so we can later find comfort in thoughts like, "I really didn't apply myself" or "I would have done better if I had spent more time on it." Although we may have found a way to deal with the fear of annihilation if rejected, we have also shielded ourselves from a full creative experience. Ironically, the less immersed we are in the project and with the audience, the more likely our efforts will fall flat and receive criticism.

There are several ways in which the threat to one's feeling of greatness can be experienced. I have been surprised to hear the same fear from almost all the artists I've worked with: "People will discover I am a fraud." The feeling that previous achievements and accomplishments were lucky or a fluke reflects the artist's vulnerability as his artistic work is judged or as he faces his next challenge. Even some of the most prolific and talented artists live with the underlying insecurity that their talents and immersive capacities are fleeting and tentative. The fear that one is really inadequate and will be "found out" on the next project seems to be very common.

Even if an artist feels she has genuine talent, she may fear not being able to live up to previous accomplishments or her reputation. The feeling that one has set a standard with previous projects that will be impossible to duplicate can paralyze further immersive attempts. The fear of being humiliated by failing to meet internal and external expectations can be crippling. One actor described having nightmares of critics describing him as a has-been and past his prime. Similarly, an illustrator described his disappointment in himself *every time* he finished a picture. Before beginning, he would visualize the completed picture in his mind. He felt his actual drawings never lived up to his initial visualization. His feeling of adequacy as an illustrator took a hit with each completed project. He felt that he ultimately did not have the skill and talent to translate to the paper what he visualized in his mind. (In reality, this illustrator is an accomplished artist who is internationally celebrated. Just goes to show how much the creative process is subjectively experienced.)

Even when a person has acquired an identity as "the talented one" or "the successful one," further immersive opportunities can be felt as a test of this title. In this way, prior successes can actually inhibit risking current immersive experiences.

The Fear of Success

Another interesting block to immersion is the fear of being too great. The fear of success can be a block in its own right and can represent a fear of change. Becoming a success often means a change in lifestyle: financial freedom opens up new potentials; new friends and colleagues emerge; and social and professional visibility can increase. Although many of these changes can be positive, success may also mean the loss of the familiar and comfortable. The creation of anything new involves the destruction of something old, which brings with it considerable anxiety.

One author I see for therapy was surprised at the shift in dynamics and power structure within her family once she became famous. She had held the role of the black sheep in her family. Her older siblings had always viewed her as the screw-up, and her parents had always labeled her the baby. Throughout her life she accepted this identity, always doubting her capacities and never really feeling like a grown-up. However, when her books began selling and she started acquiring wealth, she became very uncomfortable. Even though she was making millions of dollars, she stayed in her small $550-per-month apartment. She became very anxious when she considered buying a larger house. She also became paralyzed in writing. We eventually understood that she felt her success threatened her relationships with family members. And, indeed, her parents and siblings *were* struggling to cope with her newfound wealth and fame. They became more critical and distant from her. They were jealous of her success because it threatened their own self-worth. She felt they could not tolerate her change in position in the unspoken family hierarchy: her siblings could no longer feel better than their sister (an experience they needed to boost their self-esteem), and her parents could no longer get their sense of self-worth through taking care of their helpless, inept baby.

At one point, she felt the price for her success was too high and considered quitting writing. However, she was instead able to develop an understanding of family members' jealousy and found ways to sensitively respond to them. She also addressed her own struggle to accept her new identity and lifestyle. She was no longer a failure or a baby. This acceptance of a new identity enabled her to get past her fear-of-success block and helped her create new dynamics within her family.

The Fear of Having Nothing to Offer

One important aspect of feeling special and great is the experience of having something to offer to others. Being able to provide something to others gives us a sense of worth and value. In fact, it is this anticipation of sharing something special that provides a powerful impetus to immerse in creative endeavors.

We all need to feel that we have something special and unique to offer. We feel gratified when we can provide for our children, our peers, our students, and even our mentors. Many artists are also energized by fantasizing about having something to offer to the world. We hope to be able to communicate to others so that we may help, heal, and teach. When we are successful, our own value is enhanced, and we become more hopeful about the future.

However, the fear that we have nothing of value to offer, or that no one would be interested in our gifts, can inhibit us from immersion. If I have nothing of value to say, what's the point in speaking? Or what if I believe I have something unique to contribute, and no one else understands its value? Both anticipations of deficiency can insult our sense of specialness and inhibit our capacity for immersion.

True, we need to receive positive mirroring from others in order to be psychologically nourished. But we also need to be able to provide this nourishment *to* others in order to be psychologically gratified. In fact, sometimes it is even more gratifying to be the provider. This give-and-take between self and other, or between self and creative medium, creates a *mutuality* of interaction that underlies our strength and confidence.

Our confidence in being a trustworthy provider depends, in large part, on our personal histories and experiences. For example, consider the experience between children and parents. Parents are taught to provide for their children and not to depend on their kids to help them meet their own needs. However, although we need to be careful not to "parentify" our children by expecting them to take care of us, if we never look to them for support, we may be depriving them of the opportunity to be a valued *provider* to others. A healthy balance must exist in giving and receiving so that a child does not feel overwhelmed or burdened. Also, we must be sensitive to each individual child's experience. But a child's self-worth is enhanced when others recognize that he has something meaningful to contribute and that he is a capable giver. A person who has been able to experience being a capable and trustworthy provider to others may also feel more readily that he or she has something valuable to offer through an artistic realm.

GUIDES

1. DARE TO DREAM BIG.

Fantasies of greatness, power, and specialness propel us forward. These kinds of fantasies are the healthy foundation of our creativity, our selves, and our vitality. If it is difficult to entertain such dreams, think back to previous relationships and see if someone has deflated your dream by "being reasonable." For the "good of the child," many parents get anxious if their child expresses hopes and fantasies of greatness ("I'm going to be a rock star when I grow up"). Fearing their child will be devastated when failing to become a celebrity, and wanting to protect the child from this disappointment, they feel the responsibility to nip this fantasy in the bud. Or the parents may fear that if the child is allowed to entertain this fantasy, it might impede his pursuits in other, more "realistic" endeavors. The real harm in this well-intentioned response to a child's dream is that the child feels deflated and even humiliated for fantasizing about such a thing. Take back your dreams of childhood and then reach for them!

2. EVALUATE YOUR SUPPORT NETWORK.

Even though artists may require isolation in order to immerse, it is the presence of certain types of relationships that gives them the courage and strength to take the dive. The mere presence of other people in the artist's life does not necessarily provide the kind of support he needs. (One can feel alone in a crowd.) The kind of support an artist feels contributes to his internal sense of being special, safe, and understandable. (In fact, this applies to everyone. For any person to be at his best emotionally, cognitively, behaviorally, and physically, these kinds of interpersonal experiences are fundamental.)

3. REACH OUT FOR SUPPORT.

Do you have someone who admires and appreciates your art? Turn to him or her. Elicit his or her support. This does not have to feel like begging for a compliment. So often we are not aware of what we need from others, or if we are aware, we don't ask for it. But mental health can be viewed as being able to elicit what we need from others. It requires, first, an awareness of what it is we need and, second, being able to ask for it in a way that is likely to elicit a positive response. That means that we need to be specific in our requests, sometimes even offering a script: "I need you to tell me what is good about my project" or "I need your encouragement" or "I need you to tell me it's going to be okay" or "I need you to tell me that I can do it." More often than not, others are pleased to provide these kinds of support, and they can be invaluable sources of strength in our process.

Of course, negative feedback can be toxic to our strength and confidence, particularly when we are already feeling vulnerable. Distancing from negative or critical others may be needed. For example, many artists refuse to read reviews or critiques of their work. However, constructive critical feedback can be experienced as helpful when it follows an appreciation of the work.

4. MENTOR OR TEACH SOMEONE ELSE.

Another way to feel appreciated is to mentor or teach someone else. Strength and self-confidence are bolstered when we can teach others and feel that our skills are recognized. In addition, providing positive support to others strengthens our own sense of having something to offer.

CHAPTER FIVE

Finding Inspiration in Heroes

Ray Charles inspired me. I remember listening to his records as a teenager and being in awe of his talent. His genius. To this day, he remains my idol. My biggest dream is that he would listen to one of my recordings.

— SCOTT, SINGER AND COMPOSER

Those who do not want to imitate anything, produce nothing.

— SALVADOR DALÍ

We gain a fundamental feeling of determination and inspiration when we have someone to look up to, to admire, and to aspire to please. When our heroes (in reality or fantasy) recognize us and take us under their wing, we feel solidly supported and energized. We want to be like them and to make them proud of us. Having a hero is a strong psychological motivator from the moment of birth until the time of death.

Heinz Kohut, the father of contemporary psychology theory, believed that idealizing others is "adaptively valuable and provides lasting support to the personality." The idealized other is one who is "gazed at in awe, admired, looked up to, and like which one wants to become." Our ideals and values are acquired and internalized through the process of admiring and idealizing a powerful figure. Kohut proposed that the development of talents and skills could ultimately bridge the experiences of being perfect (the feeling of specialness described in the previous chapter) and of being less than perfect relative to others (heroes and idols). In other words, we need to be admired, praised, and valued (mirrored), as well as to feel part of and unified with figures of great strength and power.

On the one hand, having heroes provides us a sense of safety. A dream described in Rollo May's book *Man's Search for Himself* reflects our inner need for a hero: "I was in a little boat tied to a big boat. We were going through the ocean and big waves came up, piling over the sides of my boat. I wondered whether it was still tied to the big boat."

When considering how heroes help us with immersion, imagine a small child and her mother at the park. The child is playing alone in the sandbox while the mother sits nearby on a park bench. The child is immersed in play but looks back to the mother every so often, just to make sure she is still there and watching. As long as the mother is present and attentive, a glance is all the child needs to feel safe and to resume her play. But if the mother suddenly disappears, or perhaps even fails to make eye contact when the child visually checks in, the child's play stops. Without the presence and attention of the mother, the child no longer feels safe to immerse in other things. As artists, we are most free to immerse into creativity when we have an idealized other "on the bench."

On the other hand, having a hero strengthens and inspires us to action. Most artists can easily identify those who influenced their work and who have been role models and sources of inspiration. Heroes can be those who work within one's same artistic medium, thus often inspiring a style of expression or form, or they can be champions of other fields or areas, as with a writer inspired by the music of an artist or by the philosophies of a teacher.

In 1875 Auguste Rodin traveled to Florence to pay homage to sculpture's past. There on the Piazza della Signoria were great works by Donatello, Michelangelo, and Cellini. With masterpieces all around him, Rodin sought to find his place in a lineage and to learn what he called "secrets" from "magicians." Rodin subsequently became a hero to a junior sculptor, Camille Claudel, who was strengthened and inspired in her romantic affair with him. She wanted to be a sculptor in her own right, and she believed that receiving the interest of an eminent senior artist was a good sign that one day she too would be famous.

IDOLS

A further, and broader, example of how having heroes is central to building and sustaining our psychological strength is society's creation of idols and idealized figures. These larger-than-life figures (celebrities, politicians, humanitarians, etc.) inspire the common person and give us strength and hope. Rather than being silly or a sign of mental immaturity, idealizing others inspires us individually and collectively as a society.

The experience of idealizing others helps us to find our own inspiration. Having a powerful person (or God or belief or idea) to turn to when we feel vulnerable strengthens us and gives us hope and inspiration to be able to move forward. Idealizing others is actually a healthy human striving toward growth. And as we mature, these fantasies of idealization progress from primitive forms (idols are infallible and superhuman) to more mature forms of regard, respect, and admiration.

Of course, idol worship is often viewed as dysfunctional and unhealthy. Crazed fans or idol stalkers are most often desperately alone and lacking heroes in their personal lives. The hunger to be recognized by an idol leads these people to extreme measures and is usually followed by crushing disillusionment when their idol fails to live up to their fantasy. However, for most of us and more often than not, idealization is a healthy part of our inner experience and provides us the needed sense of the presence of a powerful other.

THE PRESENCE OF HEROES

Ideally, parents initially provide this needed experience of heroes for their children. Young children depend on their parents for physical and psychological care. They view the parents as bigger than life, more knowledgeable and powerful than other people. This makes sense because the young child is utterly dependent on them for her existence. In order to feel safe, she must believe that her parents are all-powerful, all-knowing, and all-loving.

It is natural for a child to want to be like and please her parents to make them proud of her. This wish spurs the child's growth, and — especially when the parent takes notice of the child's accomplishments — newly developed skills become a part of the child's own feeling of competence.

In *The Dynamics of Creation*, Anthony Storr describes how artistic talent is often apparent in childhood and

> if it is encouraged by praise of the parents, it may take on a momentum of its own, in common with other activities which have won the approval of authority. A child can be trained to accept the idea that painting or composing or writing are valuable activities in themselves, and pursue one or [the] other without ever asking himself why he does so. Mozart, for example, who had already started to compose at the age of four, must have

discovered immediately that his efforts delighted his father Leopold. No doubt other forces were at work within him; but the fact that his early efforts at composition won him so much interest and approval was reason enough for him to continue.

As the child ages, day-to-day doses of reality about the parents' limitations begin to occur. As the child gradually learns that his parents do not know everything about everything, he may feel disappointed but should not be devastated. He can accept the limits of his parents' knowledge without losing all respect for them. He can continue to admire and look to the parents for answers but will now view them more as real people rather than all-knowing and all-powerful. ("Daddy may not know how to swim the breast stroke, but he will never let me drown.") This fundamental trust in the hero becomes the prototype for later healthy relationships in the child's life.

Mentors and teachers can also be powerful figures in a child's, and later an adult's, life. When we admire a teacher, we naturally want to please him or her. Ideally, the teacher appreciates what we have to offer, reflecting our feeling of specialness and greatness. This positive reflection will shore up our inner strength so that we can then be receptive to learning from the teacher. The mentor or teacher, however, walks a fine line between giving constructive feedback in such a way as to promote the learning of additional skills and pointing out flaws in a way that leaves the learner self-conscious and inhibited about further immersion.

The optimal relationship between a student and teacher is mutual, or bidirectional. When the teacher can immerse in the student's project of learning, that is, allowing himself to enter into the student's inner world and appreciating what the student is thinking, feeling, and/or producing, he becomes a source of strength and support for learning to occur. With this support, the student is able to immerse into the teacher's project of teaching, that is, to allow herself to absorb the skills, thoughts, and perceptions of the teacher. This mutual responsiveness creates a safe and enduring platform from which to dive into learning.

A television documentary about the Juilliard School in New York provides a wonderful example of how the power of heroes facilitates the students' creativity. First, the relationships between the faculty and the students are intense. The faculty members are all distinguished, accomplished artists — very easily admired by reputation alone. The individual attention given to each student also adds to the intensity of the admiration experience. It seems that the students' desire to please their mentors becomes the driving force behind their grueling program, twelve to sixteen hours a day, six days a week. But the experience for the students, although mentally and physically exhausting, is exhilarating. They feel themselves growing in their skills and expertise. And more than anything else they feel supported in immersion.

Faculty members describe how they try to help their students speak in their own voices through their art. It is clear that the faculty members become deeply immersed in their students' artistry. Here is the magic of having heroes: mentors inspire these already brilliantly talented young artists toward ever-increasing self-expression and artistic engagement. The faculty is there not so much to teach skills as to help the students immerse.

In effect, the teachers create a play space with the students, where they can leave their inhibitions behind and delve into the immersive realm. Students' talents and skills are already recognized, and although they hone these as well, the main education is practicing and developing the capacity to immerse in their art.

The immersive space created between teacher and student supports each person's creativity. In a productive spiral upward, the talented students grow as artists and the teachers are personally and professionally enhanced. Many Juilliard students go on to become big-name artists. In interviews with some of these alumni, they recall their experiences with their mentors as vivid and profound. Each describes the experience at Juilliard as intense and life altering, and each remembers individual faculty members as having huge influences on the evolution of their artistry.

The experience of having a supportive, admired figure is necessary for immersion. Whenever I have been involved in a project, I have gotten much of my courage to continue through my heroes and idols. And I have found them in many areas: my parents, my husband, my professional mentor, my therapist, and even a famous musician (who I secretly hope will read my book and call me).

All of these powerful figures have given me the strength and courage to immerse myself in this project. My wish to be like them and to please them is part of what propels me forward.

Some of my admired figures are very much in my life. I proudly hand over each chapter I write to my parents, my husband, and my professional mentor. The strength I receive from being seen and recognized by them and from their wise comments gives me the courage to reenter the immersive process. It is somewhat embarrassing to admit how much strength and vitality I get from my *imaginary* relationship with the admired other, the famous musician. I have immersed in the music of this singer-songwriter for twenty-five years, and he has inspired me through several projects. (Okay, it's Peter Gabriel.) The fantasy of impressing him with this book is an incentive for me to keep writing. Maybe I could even give him some valuable insights!

As I have noted, being able to offer something to someone we admire is a profound experience. The child who is able to teach her parent something new or to comfort the parent in a time of pain is enhanced by having something valuable to offer. I recall an experience between my two-year-old niece and her father. Mark was watching a football game on TV, and Emma was playing beside him. When his football team fumbled the ball, Mark groaned out loud. Emma got up from her play, put her arms around her father's neck, and soothed him, "Its okay, Daddy. It's only a game." Mark accepted her gesture of comfort, hugging her back, saying, "You're right; that's a big help." Emma strutted back to her own game, obviously feeling proud of being able to make her daddy feel better. If he had rejected her efforts to console him (out of a belief that children should not have to comfort the parents — "I should take care of myself"), Emma would have felt diminished in her capabilities to provide for someone else.

BLOCKS AND FEARS

I have described how having a hero, someone to look up to and admire, not only supports our ability to immerse into creativity by helping us to feel safe and secure but also constitutes part of our ongoing subconscious flow of feelings about our sense of connection in the world. When we have a solid internal or external connection with a powerful other, we are apt to be inspired and motivated to strive forward. But what kinds of experiences get in our way of being able to find and experience heroes in this productive way? The following are blocks and fears we can face in developing healthy connections with heroes and in experiencing them as an aid to immersion into our own individuality and creativity.

Absence of a Parental Hero and Disillusionment

There are few experiences so devastating as the disillusionment that follows when an idealized figure betrays or neglects us. Unfortunately, some people do not have someone to admire and respect. This can result from an absence of trustworthy people in a person's life; a history of severe disappointments by others will lead to deep feelings of distrust. People who cannot trust that anyone will be strong and protective of them were usually traumatically hurt or disappointed by their parents or other caregivers in childhood. If a child experiences abuse or neglect by his parents, he is caught in a horrible dilemma. On the one hand, he has to depend on the parents for his physical and emotional survival. On the other hand, he experiences repeated disappointments and danger with the people who are supposed to keep him safe. How does the child resolve this terrible dilemma?

The child often resorts to fantasy. He develops an ability to split off the painful experiences from his awareness, memory, or feelings. By compartmentalizing experiences of abuse or neglect, the child can preserve a fantasy of the parent as strong and protective, even though this fantasy is not grounded in reality. The unconscious choice the child makes to preserve a perception of the parents as reliable and protective is necessary for his psychological survival. This choice is not a deliberate one. The mind learns to bend or distort the truth, or the child creates explanations and excuses for his parents' bad behavior, often blaming himself for causing the abuse or neglect. Although this strategy helps the child to maintain the fantasy that his parents will protect him, it sets the stage for psychological troubles as he gets older.

As this child grows up, he is likely to anticipate similar experiences with other potentially admirable figures. He will approach relationships with distrust or with a feeling of being small, powerless, and defective. If he is lucky, he will find another adult who truly is reliable and safe (perhaps another family member, a teacher, or a coach). This new relationship can help to correct his assumptions that powerful people are dangerous or his self-view that he is a problem child who deserves punishment. But remnants of the pain he experienced with his parents will be lodged in the deeper layers of his mind. He may be unconsciously waiting to be disappointed or hurt by others, or alternatively, he may blindly trust and depend entirely on a new person for perfect protection and security. Either way, the new connection is helpful but is ultimately tentative and fragile.

Often, abused children grow up feeling cheated, angry, and fearful. Their core trust has been shattered. They struggle along the best they can, trying to find strong people to count on but feeling fearful at the same time of being disappointed and betrayed again. Sadly, many of these children will fall into the hands of other abusive or unreliable adults. These experiences then validate their assumption that no one is safe or there to protect them. Finding physical and psychological survival through self-sufficiency (relying on no one) becomes the name of the game. There is no safe space for immersion. At least not with people.

For example, Franz Kafka is believed to have attributed almost magical powers to his father throughout his entire life yet never felt he received from him the acknowledgment and recognition for which he so dearly longed. Kafka's book *The Trial* seems to express his own overwhelming sense of guilt and shame from always being made to feel inadequate and in the wrong in comparison with his father. Even though we could see Kafka's artistic efforts as partly driven by an unhealthy quest for recognition from a toxic parent, it was his continued hope of being seen and heard by others through his writing that sustained his creative process.

There is probably some truth in the stereotype of the tortured, isolated artist. Many injured people turn to art for their experience of immersion because they have learned not to rely on others; relationships have been dangerous and unreliable. This is done out of self-preservation. Their real-life experiences, especially with powerful others (those who were *supposed* to be protective and caring), turned out to be traumatic disappointments. They have lost their trust that immersion with people is safe. However, hidden within this solution of turning away from people is often the deeper, healthy longing and hope to be recognized by others and to make someone proud of them through their art.

People can be quite creative in dealing with these experiences of disappointment. These same people who have lost their trust in humanity often use fantasy and imagination to create a safe relationship with a powerful figure in order to help them along in their creative process. These fantasies are tendrils of health and hope. One client of mine, a composer, who was badly abused as a child and had withdrawn into his music, described admiring the late Jerry Garcia of the Grateful Dead. He told of having imaginary conversations with Jerry about his current compositions. (These conversations were not psychotic; the artist was not hearing voices. But even if they had been psychotic hallucinations, I would have been encouraged as a therapist that this artist still held hope of being heard and understood and would have understood the content of the hallucinations as reflecting the healthy strivings of the artist's psyche.) This man could visualize these collaborations so vividly that the fantasy became a vital part of his creative process. In effect, he created an imaginary relationship with a powerful figure he admired because he could not trust anyone in his real life to be supportive and safe. This fantasy helped him through many stages of his work. He found that the strength he gained in his imaginary relationship helped him to continually reenter immersive states in composing. He also used the fantasy for nourishment of his own sense of greatness: Jerry Garcia thought he was the best composer still alive!

Many people who live solitary lives generate this important experience in some way. Spirituality is a common solution. Feeling connected to and protected by a higher power can provide the strength and security they are lacking. It is interesting, though, how the nature of the relationship they imagine with a higher power often mimics the relationship they had with their parents. Many people from abusive backgrounds imagine that God is judgmental and a presence to be feared. However, even this fearful perception provides them the psychological experience of having someone watching over them and fuels their attempts to be "good enough" and the wish to please. I have witnessed many people's perception of God shift from judgmental and controlling to understanding and compassionate through the course of psychotherapy. This shift seems directly related to the impact of the therapy relationship. Once, and if, they are able to experience me as a safe, reliable, and caring presence, they begin to be able to imagine and trust that other strong figures can also be nurturing and supportive.

Compliance

Sometimes, in the quest to please an admired other, a person will sacrifice his own individuality for the sake of the relationship. Complying with the needs and expectations of the powerful person can sometimes feel like the only way to sustain the relationship. When the admired person has specific requirements for approval (or is perceived that way), we are forced to choose between honoring the demands and losing the relationship. The importance of the approval of the admired person makes this a very difficult choice, and many of us will choose to comply rather than to risk disapproval or rejection.

As an example, say that a powerful business owner expects his son to take over the business when he retires. The father expects the son to attend business school despite the fact that the son has a dream of being a teacher. The son, who cannot risk disappointing his father for fear that the father will reject him, swallows his dream and goes to business school. Even though he does quite well in the program and eventually takes over the business, his professional life feels empty. He does not immerse in the experience but continues on this path because he desperately needs his father's approval.

D. W. Winnicott wrote extensively about compliance, noting that the creative sense "more than anything else makes the individual feel that life is worth living. Contrasted with this is a relationship to external reality which is one of compliance. . . . Playing and creativity is the opposite of compliance." He goes on to say that when compliance dominates a person's relationships, that person develops what he calls a false self-organization. The false self "always lacks something, and that something is the *essential element of creative originality*."

This is not to say that all compliance is bad or that one should never comply with the needs of others. Compliance can be a gratifying experience when a person chooses to try to meet the needs of another. But it is when we feel that we must always give up our own needs and uniqueness in order to satisfy someone else's expectations that it becomes toxic to our creative process. When a person does not feel that she has a choice (the risks are too high, such as the loss of an important relationship), compliance becomes a cage that does not allow for freedom of immersion. I will discuss this idea further in chapter 7, as it relates to considering the audience and their needs and desires.

Rebellion and Rage

At the other end of the continuum from compliance are rebellion and rage. Rather than understanding these as a primary, instinctual drive, contemporary psychology theory views rebellion and rage as by-products of disillusionment and betrayal by others. They reflect the individual's attempts to regain power and to punish the offender. Their energy comes from a wish for revenge and a need to restore one's sense of control and justice in the interpersonal environment.

Actually, the artistic expression of rebellion or rage indicates that the artist still has hope of being heard and understood. If we have given up on being heard, appreciated, and understood, we sink into a state of helplessness and despair. It is not worth the effort to express our discontent if we have no hope of being heard.

Artists who are inspired to express their disappointments and hurts through aggressive content and form still have enough hope to fight — to vigorously assert their point of view, their independence, or their internal experience. Their artwork may be the only medium that gives them a voice, enabling them to stand up to others.

GUIDES

I. DEVELOP RELATIONSHIPS WITH THOSE YOU ADMIRE.

Do you have a mentor, teacher, or other admired person to look up to? The strength you receive through being taken under the wing of someone strong and safe can be a powerful support in creative immersion. If you have such a figure, either in reality or as a fantasy, use him when you are in need of support. Connect with him. If you have an admired figure in reality, ask for her advice, her feedback, and her help. Being able to ask for support is a sign of strength and will sustain your creative process. Be specific in your requests. "What do you do when you are blocked?" or "How do you deal with your fears?" or "Have you ever felt the way that I do?" or "Will you help me by giving me some positive feedback?" Most mentors feel honored and pleased to offer such support.

2. IMMERSE IN THE WORK OF SOMEONE YOU RESPECT.

If you are inspired by the work of a particular artist, connect with that person by immersing in her work (read her books, listen to her music, appreciate her art, etc.). Whatever originally inspired you in her work, which developed into your respect and admiration for the artist, will probably inspire and strengthen you again.

3. MAKE USE OF FANTASY HEROES.

Call up your hero or idol in fantasy. Imagine meeting your hero and showing him your work. Imagine that your hero appreciates your work, hears its message, and supports your continued efforts. Also, imagine your hero facing creative blocks or procrastination. What would your hero do? (A shorthand: wwyhd?)

CHAPTER SIX

Finding Comfort in Twins

I was amazed and deeply comforted. I went to this meeting of writers; it was really more of a social event. And here were authors who were hugely successful, prolific writers. And they struggled the same way that I struggle! I couldn't believe that they felt the same insecurities, the same doubts about their work — and their selves! I have never felt so understood. Maybe I am not so crazy after all. Maybe these feelings come with the territory.

— JULIE, AUTHOR

A third kind of relationship that helps us immerse into creativity is being with "like-kind." Here we find the experience of being with others who are in the same boat. Relationships with "twins" help us feel understood and understandable; our feelings and experiences make sense and we find comfort in the awareness that we are all alike. Our fantasies, fears, and dreams are acceptable. Our blocks, resistances, and failures do not mean we are inadequate to the task; we can go on in spite of our fears because we are not alone. Because these relationships give us the feeling that we are not alone in our efforts and that we share the same feelings and struggles with people who are just like us, I refer to them as "twinship relationships."

My brother offered me a powerful experience of twinship that helped me begin to write this book. He is a professor and the author of three academic books. When I told him I was planning to write this book, he immediately knew what thoughts and feelings I was having: Am I expert enough to write a book? Do I have something valid to say or am I fooling myself? Is what I want to say so obvious that people reading the book will say, "Yeah, so?" Hearing him echo my own concerns was extremely comforting. "So this is the process that every writer goes through," I thought. Knowing he experienced similar insecurities and still managed to write books helped me to avoid paralysis in starting. He offered me many tips on how to enter the project. And with every concern I expressed, his giggle of acknowledgment, followed by advice or resonance, helped me to know that I was not weird and that my concerns did not mean that I wasn't up to writing a book. My fears were all too familiar to him because he had been there countless times. This connection with him helped me to begin writing *despite* my insecurities and uncertainties. I have continued to turn to this twinship connection with my brother throughout my writing experience. I call him when I get stuck or when I begin to doubt the entire project. His responses of "Oh, I know" or "I'm feeling the same thing with my book right now" are powerful antidotes to the blocks to immersion that I encounter.

The importance of twinship relationships to our mental health has been recognized in the psychological literature. Heinz Kohut viewed twinship experiences (or "alter-ego" experiences, as he called them) as one of the important pillars of the self. In fact, researchers working with monkeys and apes have similarly observed the powerful role that peer relationships play in their psychological development and healthy functioning.

Harry Harlow, PhD, a psychologist who conducted experiments in the 1960s and 1970s with rhesus monkeys, discovered that "the interaction of a baby monkey with its contemporaries was more important to the animal's future ability to mate successfully, and also, in the case of a female, to become a satisfactory mother, than the baby's relationship with its mother." We should also note that a baby monkey learns to interact with its contemporaries chiefly through different types of play.

In another study, rhesus monkey infants were separated from their mothers at birth. They were brought up in partial social isolation, where they could see but could not touch other monkeys. They showed a great increase in fear of other monkeys when finally allowed to mix with them. They displayed aggressive behavior toward the other monkeys, toward the researchers by biting the experimenter's glove as they were being fed, and toward themselves by biting their own arms and legs.

However, somewhat surprisingly, monkeys who had been separated from their mothers at birth but were allowed to mix with other infant monkeys developed pretty normally. It seemed that mixing with contemporaries largely made up for the maternal deprivation. By contrast, when the babies were allowed contact with only their mothers, and not other infants, for the first seven months of their lives, and the infants were only then allowed to come together, they did not play normally. The best mothering could not compensate for the deprivation of play with contemporaries.

Although it pains me to know about monkeys being treated this way by humans, it does help us to understand the usefulness of human peer support groups. Connecting with others who are experiencing the same things is very comforting and strengthening. We feel less alone, and this can free us to be more playful. Finding others who understand because they are going through the same thing is a special kind of connection that can be felt only with peers.

Twinship relationships can also be very helpful in boosting our courage to immerse into creativity, comforting us when we are stressed, and encouraging us when we are filled with self-doubt.

Many writers belong to writing groups, for example. Being with others who are involved in the same process can help one to feel strong enough to reenter immersive states. This can happen because the group itself can become an immersive experience, another immersive realm where we get psychologically fortified so that our creativity and hope are stirred.

An intense twinship-and-love relationship between the writers Anaïs Nin and Henry Miller in the 1930s fueled the artistic capacities of both. The two shared ideas, quotations, essays, and books. They read and criticized each other's work. They both noted the "equality" of their relationship and, even though their styles were vastly different, their relationship provided mutual enrichment of each other's intellectual and artistic capacities. Nin said in "Djuna," "I imagined many books born out of our intimacy," and they were, in the words of Philip Jason, "soulmates, fleshmates, unique contributors to one another's very different paths as writers."

ENSEMBLE ARTISTS

Not only do twinship relationships help solo artists immerse in artistic work, but this type of relationship is fundamental to ensemble work. Ensemble artists, such as dancers, actors, and instrumentalists, rely on twinship experiences to generate the collective artistic product. In ensemble groups, the creative "play space" is found in the relational space among its members. Although each artist contributes his individual talents and creativity, the individual efforts are channeled into a mutual relational space that generates an artistic creation that is more than the sum of its parts. At their best, ensemble projects involve the ultimate experience of twinship: each member is enhanced by relationships in the group, which allows for a collective immersion in the project at hand.

However, as in any group experience, there are blocks and obstacles to experiencing and sustaining the kinds of harmonious twinship relationships that generate optimal creativity. To be able to experience optimal twinship relationships, all members of the group must feel that they are equal. I think of the dynamics of the cast of the TV program *Friends*. The actors all agreed to insist on equal pay for their work. They realized that if one of them was paid more than the others, this would lead to individual feelings of competitiveness and resentment and would break down the sense of group cohesion. Through this agreement, they were able to successfully retain the group experience of equality and sameness that is critical for twinship relationships.

Another important aspect of sustaining twinship relationships in an ensemble is to be able to maintain an individual identity. Although these relationships are built on a feeling of equality, each person must be able to retain an independent identity and value within the group. Clearly defining the roles within the group or within the project helps support the unique talents and identities of its members. If members feel that their individual talents are not recognized (reflecting their feelings of greatness and specialness) or that the group identity threatens to wipe out their individual identities as artists, then they will become defensive and self-protective and lose the ability to immerse in group creativity. Respecting the need for individual expression within the group is often achieved through solos or by allowing each person a particular niche of the project. In addition to preserving each member's individual identity, this type of structure also allows each member to have control over certain pieces of the project that do not have to be compromised with or influenced by others. When this balance between individual creativity and group creativity can be established, ensemble experience and creation can be profoundly gratifying.

BLOCKS AND FEARS

What gets in our way of developing and sustaining twinship relationships? Let's examine some of the possible blocks and fears that inhibit us from experiencing twinship.

Absence of Twinship Relationships in Childhood

Twinship, as noted, is that experience of being with like-kind. Siblings, friends, and peers can all provide that sense of alikeness or sameness with others. It is important to experience twinship relationships, because they make us feel understandable and sane and give us a feeling of belonging. When our thoughts, feelings, and behaviors are mutually shared with others, we begin to feel part of a larger group. When we face similar challenges alongside our peers, the understanding and empathy generated among group members can be a powerful source of strength. We need to feel that we are connected — we must identify with others and sense that they identify with us.

Some people readily seek out and establish these kinds of relationships. This resourcefulness probably stems from successful early childhood experiences of twinship: the child had siblings or peer groups available that were appropriate and provided a goodness of fit. Within these relationships, the child experienced himself as being like others and came to trust and anticipate feeling included in a group. The child developed a strong foundation of trust. "We are all the same" became a believable and a powerful source of strength.

However, some people do not enjoy such group experiences as children. For many reasons, a compatible peer group may not have been available to them. And it couldn't be just any peer group: the others must be a good fit with the child's temperament, physical and emotional abilities, and, often, life circumstance to foster a sense of twinship. If a child has a unique talent or deficiency, he may not experience twinship with children who do not share this trait. In fact, in mismatched peer groups, this child may feel painfully *different* from the others. If the child does not feel that others in the group share the same struggles, challenges, and joys, it will not be a twinship experience and can leave the child feeling alone and different.

A person who does not experience twinship as a child may have a difficult time developing these relationships as an adult. This person will have already established an identity of being different and may have a difficult time reaching out to others for this kind of support. Tentative and hesitant, this person may be fearful of exposing his differentness and retreat from peer and intimate relationships. In addition, this fear of exposure may inhibit his artistic endeavors because of his fear of standing out.

Competitiveness

Competition among peers can be a facilitating or an inhibiting force. A competitive spirit can propel many people to reach beyond their comfort zone, as they witness others like them enjoying the fruits of immersion. Seeing others take a successful dive can strengthen a person's hope that he, too, can risk and achieve. Not wanting to be left alone at water's edge, a person may stretch beyond his fears in order to keep up with others. In this way, competitive experiences can increase the hope one feels for a new beginning.

I have had a positive experience of this dynamic in a study group to which I have belonged for a number of years. The group is made up of psychologists and is facilitated by a senior psychiatrist we all admire. We share an interest in contemporary psychoanalysis and meet monthly to discuss clinical material and theoretical ideas. Over the years, we have formed close friendships extending beyond our meetings, so that our twinship experience with each other is both professional and personal. Over time, we have come to trust each other and have been increasingly able to immerse with each other. We are able to present our clinical ideas and clinical interactions openly and honestly: our interest has shifted from merely impressing each other to really using each other as a source of creativity and growth.

The positive competitive spirit that has developed within the group has propelled each of us toward increased immersion in our psychotherapy, as well as in academic and artistic realms. When we saw one of our group succeed in writing and presenting a paper at the annual international conference, each of us felt an increased sense of competence: "We are all the same, so if Todd could do it, then we all can do it." Since Todd's original paper, each of us has created something of our own to contribute professionally. The twinship experience we enjoy has largely increased the capacity of each of us to risk immersion through the supportive competitive spirit that exists among us.

However, competitiveness can also inhibit a person's capacity to risk immersion. Fearing not being able to keep up, a person may retreat from the competition and from the experience of twinship itself. This can happen when the goal of the competition becomes performance rather than process and insecurities about competence and not being good enough are felt. A person with fragile self-confidence may become frightened and lose the experience of twinship. ("I'm really not like them after all.") Once again alone, this person is not likely to risk immersion, as the dread to repeat old injuries is stronger than the hope for a new beginning. The perceived risk of failing in competition with one's peers can be very threatening to self-esteem. It is safer to withdraw from the competition, and, thus, the twinship relationship, than to risk annihilation of self-esteem and self-confidence.

The difference between experiencing competitiveness as enhancing or inhibiting is complex. Many factors come into play: the nature of the fit between or among "twins," the psychological strength and resilience of each member, the nature of the competition (goal or process), and the outcomes of one's previous experiences with competition. One of the challenges throughout our lives is to find and create twinship relationships that balance this hope and dread and provide us with a strengthening experience of standing at water's edge, side by side.

GUIDES

I. SEEK OUT TWINSHIP RELATIONSHIPS.

Do you have the presence of a twinship group or other "like-kind" relationship? Finding (or creating) a support group of people doing the same thing, confronting similar fears, and generally sharing the same process can be invaluable. Within such a group, you can experience that you are not alone, that your fears are not unique, and that others are struggling and succeeding. These groups can be developed through taking classes, over the Internet, or through other artistic associations. Pulling together or joining a writer's group, or other similar artistically focused group, can sustain you through the creative process. Or join a psychotherapy support group to deal with deeper fears and blocks you may be encountering.

2. EXPLORE YOUR PAST HISTORY WITH TWINSHIP RELATIONSHIPS.

What was your experience in finding peer groups as a child? Did you have negative experiences that blocked your hope for a future experience of belonging? Recall a time when you did feel the same as others. What was the foundation of your feeling of sameness? How did you feel different? Although nobody is exactly alike, chances are your experience is very similar to that of other artists.

CHAPTER SEVEN

Connecting with the Audience and Meeting Deadlines

Although I think human relationships are the most important to me, I don't think I could survive without musical and visual stimulation. My order of priorities is: my heart, my ears and my eyes. I believe there is a ritualistic aspect to all performances, just by the nature of the stage and an audience and the exaggeration that provides for gestures. Sometimes, by moving very slowly and deliberately, one can pinpoint a mood in a way that draws people into the music. When I go to a concert, I want to be moved and excited by passion and imagination. That is my aim as a performer.

—— PETER GABRIEL, *PETER GABRIEL*

The difference between artistic self-expression and creating a work of art is engagement with the audience. In creating a work of art, the artist is reaching out for the audience, attempting to convey or communicate a feeling, experience, or idea. The artist is hoping to touch the audience in some way, to elicit a certain kind of response from them.

After all, each of us hopes that our audience will hear our message and will ultimately understand and enter into our artistic experience. We hope to be able to communicate with others so that we feel appreciated and understood as well as to offer something of value to them. In order to achieve this, you must integrate them into your project. You need to stay in connection with them throughout your creative process. Through your fantasies and assumptions about the audience, you must find a language or artistic form they will understand. Without these considerations of the audience, performances or works of art can fail to engage others. Although the audience may be impressed that you are doing your own thing, they may find it difficult to understand or to share in the immersive connection. In this scenario, the audience remains on the outside of the artwork, observing it rather than being invited into it.

The nature of your engagement with the audience throughout the creative process is largely determined by what perceptions you have about them. The assumptions that you make about who the audience is, what they need and want, and what they expect from you will determine how much you are able to incorporate them into your creative process. Will they be appreciative? Will they be approving, admiring, generous, and loving? Or will they be critical, hostile, withholding, and stingy? Your assumptions about the audience can be like an ink blot test. (What does the ink blot look like to *you*?) Because the idea of an audience is a vague, abstract entity, you are likely to project your own hopes and fears about your assumed place with others onto that audience.

Another reality for artists is dealing with deadlines. When we are involved in making art to share with others, we must often work within externally determined time frames. Making deadlines can be a tricky challenge: our capacity to create within someone else's time frame is influenced by our assumptions about what it is to be with others and how to maintain our sense of self within the connection.

ASSUMPTIONS ABOUT THE AUDIENCE

The assumptions you make about the audience are generated from your previous experiences and from your hopeful fantasies of future experience. You tend to assume that your previous encounters with audiences will be repeated. So, if a singer has previously been applauded and acknowledged in her performance, she will likely anticipate future positive response. Fantasizing that the next audience will also be appreciative and affirming, she will feel safer about integrating them into her creative process. But if she has received poor or hostile responses from a previous audience, she will likely anticipate that the next audience will also be critical. This anticipation of a negative response will either halt her creative process or cause her to split off or cut out the idea of the audience. In order to preserve her ability to safely immerse herself in her artwork, she may need to deny that the audience exists or that the audience's response matters to her at all.

Sometimes an artist will need to deny the existence of the audience so that he can continue his work. Loren Long, the illustrator I interviewed and presented in chapter 3, described needing to do just that in order to create his paintings. He told me this story about being chosen to do the illustration for Madonna's book *Mr. Peabody's Apples*.

Loren's agent called to tell him that he was to go to New York to meet with Madonna's publisher. When he arrived, he learned that he was their first choice to illustrate her book but the contract was not yet guaranteed. He was assigned to do a test painting to win or lose the project. Specific instructions were given to pay special attention to the facial features of the characters. Madonna would then decide on the basis of his submission if Loren was a good fit.

Instead of leaving the meeting with a contract in hand as he had anticipated, he was leaving with anxiety about passing a test. He was tense and riddled with self-doubt on his plane ride home. He described feeling the experience as surreal. After all, this was Madonna, one of the most famous people in the world. He became anxious about Madonna and her publisher evaluating his work. He decided right then that he could not consider his audience at all. He consciously blocked them out. "I knew it would have been difficult to draw with that pressure. I told myself that this project would be business as usual and that helped me to relax. I just have to do what I do."

Once he had blocked Madonna from his mind, he confronted another problem, for upon his first reading of her manuscript, he had already envisioned the most climactic picture for the book. But the problem was that his image did not show faces. He struggled with what to submit: should he follow the requirements and change his visions about what the picture should be, or should he follow his own creative instincts and create what was in his mind? He decided to be true to himself, accepting that drawing the picture without faces could result in rejection.

Once he decided to paint the picture the way he had envisioned it, he was able to enjoy his process and complete the painting. To his delight, Madonna loved his work, and he was chosen for the project. He found that once he had been chosen, he was less intimidated by her megastar status. He felt she was already in his corner, and he was able to integrate her feedback and ideas throughout the actual process of illustrating the book.

MAKING ASSUMPTIONS

In addition to actual previous experiences with audiences, another way we develop assumptions about the audience is through our history with personal relationships. Fundamentally, these assumptions about what to expect with and from others are formed in childhood.

New research on parent-infant interaction suggests that the way parents relate with their child forms the child's prototype of relationships throughout life. In other words, these early life interactions with the parents organize the child's assumptions about what to expect from others, what he has to offer to others, and his perceived safety of immersing with people in general. The basic flow, rhythm, and emotional tone of these interactive moments form the basis for what the child expects in other relationships and determine how the child is likely to behave in relation with another person.

For example, say a child's creativity and play are usually met with enthusiasm and participation by her parents. This child's prototype of immersing into an activity includes receiving appreciation from others and feeling a connection with them. She feels free to move in and out of immersive spaces and does not feel inhibited by the presence of others. She does not need to erect self-preserving defenses because she does not anticipate rejection or dismissal. And on the occasion when she is disappointed (her parents do not join in with her play), she experiences this break as out of the norm and is able to bounce back resiliently and quickly.

Through moments like these, a child acquires a basic building block of what it is like to be with another person. Accumulating these blocks in many interactions with the parents builds the child's basic assumptions about what to expect in relationships throughout life. If moments of shared enthusiasm occur regularly and often, the child comes to expect this response and feels safe enough to allow immersion with others.

As adults, we continue to be psychologically organized by these early interactions. Most of us do not consciously recognize the patterns we repeat over and over in relationships and how most of these patterns are a result of unconscious assumptions we make about the anticipated response of the "other." As artists, we make these same assumptions about our audience and behave in ways that re-create the basic patterns of interactions from our childhood.

Once we become aware of these assumptions, we can do a reality check to determine if they are still valid. For example, one of my artist clients described how his mother never played with him. He developed a prototype (or average expectable experience) of being alone when he played. He assumed that other people would not play with him, so he quit asking. When he became an artist, he assumed that his audience wouldn't be interested either, so he didn't consider them in his creative process. It didn't occur to him that their response mattered. Reality check: His mother was depressed when he was young. She could barely make it out of bed each day. Maybe other people would have enjoyed playing with him, but he had given up and had withdrawn himself. Maybe his audience would be interested. He needed to risk being rejected and give them a chance. After all, all he had ever really wanted was a playmate.

The patterns of our anticipated interactions with others developed in childhood remain unchanged until current experiences replace them. These original prototypes can be modified and changed when either person in the relationship acts differently than in the original script. So, even if our original prototypes of interactions with others involved feeling rejected or dismissed, we have the potential to develop more positive interactions, but *only if* we understand how our reflexive, self-protective positions help to re-create and maintain the old patterns. We must risk new ways of reaching out for support from others and eliciting our desired response from them. This certainly applies to our personal relationships, but it is also relevant in our considerations of our relationship with our audience.

An interesting variation of an artist's connection with the audience is illustrated by another one of my clients. She is shy and insecure in her personal relationships but feels confident and secure in her artistic relationships. In her interpersonal relationships, she learned to anticipate rejection or dismissal. So in her personal relationships she protects herself by erecting protective shields and barriers. But when she expressed herself artistically, she received praise and acknowledgment. Her self-confidence as an artist and her ability to engage with the audience are built on her prototypes of positive responses to her artwork. Creative activities became her safe place, a place that she can be with others and feel hopeful for interpersonal connection.

In such a case, it is easy to understand how artistic expression is crucial to sustaining this artist's sense of self. She can get filled up by experiencing longed-for and needed immersive moments with an audience. However, the strength and hope that she experiences with an audience do not necessarily cross over into her personal life. She has developed two distinct, parallel assumptions about her place with others: the artist self, who is strong and hopeful, and the personal self, who is frightened and alone. This artist feels that without her art, she is nothing.

This type of development of parallel identities usually begins in childhood. Artists who have such a split experience often began artistic expression and performance at a young age. The development of their artist self actually occurred alongside the development of their personal self. Thus, both selves develop, mature, and grow, but each can hold very different assumptions and expectations about relationships. It is often quite jarring to learn that some of our most idolized celebrity figures, who seem so confident and "together," suffer terribly in their personal lives. They may turn to drugs and other substances or suffer depression as a result of this inability to transfer the strength they gain through artistic immersion into their personal lives and personal self.

Although Jackson Pollock was a prolific artist who confidently broke through boundaries of previous notions of visual art, in his personal life he suffered frequent depressions and bouts with alcohol abuse. Except for a few years when he was able to intimately connect with his fellow artist and lover Lee Krasner (and this was also the period in which he began to create the work that made him the first internationally famous modern painter in America), Pollock was socially awkward, depressed, and alienated. He suffered severe self-doubt and displayed a volatile temper. Despite the acclaim and recognition he received as a painter, I would say that his inability to form and sustain personal relationships eventually prevented his creative immersion and ultimately led to his suicide.

Another example is one of my clients, Susan, an acclaimed classical pianist, who began to take lessons as a young girl. She was naturally gifted at piano and received awards throughout her childhood and adolescence. She was a confident, bold, and expressive pianist and looked forward to the thrill of competitions and recitals. However, personally, she was shy, withdrawn, and socially awkward. She had overwhelming social anxiety in her personal life. Her pianist self grew up in a vital world of mirrors (she received praise and recognition from others for her playing), of heroes (she had several idealizable teachers who took her under their wing), and of twins (she was comfortable in her music classes and playfully competed with her peers). But outside the world of music, she felt invisible and insecure.

As a child, her parents focused on her talent. Although she had always felt them to be supportive of her music, she also carried a sense of responsibility to become great: Susan's mother, who was also a talented musician but had given up her career to help support the family, needed Susan to make up for her sacrifice. Her father, a workaholic, was rarely home but would come to her recitals and competitions. Outside of the music world, her parents were both emotionally and physically unavailable to her. Her pianist self grew and developed in a healthy way, while her personal self was alone, frightened, and insecure.

Our therapeutic relationship tended to her personal self. Although she was thirty-two when she came to see me, she seemed more like a little girl — I found myself drawn to mother this fragile and frightened child sitting in front of me. I bridged her split development by acknowledging my admiration and respect for her musical talents and accomplishments, and then quickly moving on to connect with her personal experience. I empathized with how alone she had felt outside of her music world. I found myself naturally interacting with her in a way I would with a small child — tuning in to her obvious anxiety and self-doubt and attempting to hold her in a way with words that were soothing and reassuring. I tended to her personal self, carefully eliciting and listening to her thoughts, feelings, and questions about relationships, body image, and romance. She was hesitant to fully engage with me at first, saying that she was fearful that she would connect with me and then I would leave her.

Through many sessions, I could visually see her increasing self-strength. She began to present herself with much more vitality and confidence. Her speaking voice became stronger and she spoke more directly and clearly. The nature of our interactions shifted as well. I realized she was no longer eliciting a purely mirroring response from me. She was curious about me and my practice and began to reach out for a twinship connection about creativity and music.

She joined a gym in order to start exercising and met a woman there who became a friend — the first friend she had ever had outside of the music world. Through this friendship and our continued therapeutic relationship, she began to blossom as a young woman. Her personal self was finally being integrated with her pianist self, each adding a mutual spark to the other.

THE SELF IN CONNECTION

The ultimate challenge in engaging with an other, whether that is another person or an audience, is retaining our own sense of self while still responding to the needs of the other. Most people struggle to find and sustain this balance. In considering his relationship with his audience, an artist may vacillate between extreme positions on this continuum. At the one end, he is most concerned with self-preservation: "I do what I do, and the audience can like it or lump it. I refuse to tailor my artistic expression, even slightly, to their needs or expectations because I would be selling myself out." At the other extreme, the only mission is meeting audience demand: "What I do is only as valuable as the audience's response to it. I must give them what they want."

Neither of these extreme positions leads to an immersive experience for the artist or the audience. Each involves a negation of one of the partners in the relationship. The artist will cease to be truly creative if he is merely fulfilling a formula for audience approval. In this case, the lack of the artist's creative immersion leads to shallowness in the art. And when the artist totally dismisses the presence and needs of the audience, he is likely to lose the connection that channels his expression to them. He may feel safe from criticism and rejection, but he is alone and misses out on the gratification found in the immersive connection with others.

Ideally, the artist and the audience engage in a mutual relationship. In this case, both the artist and the audience are present and respected. Both can exist independently within the connection. The artist is immersed in her artwork and invites the audience into her space. She considers the audience, their likes and dislikes, and speaks to them. She uses an artistic language and form that will likely be understood and appreciated. And in return, the audience responds. Through their appreciative response and feedback, the artist feels special and validated. This support bolsters her courage to immerse further into her artwork and further with the audience. This is a mutually gratifying experience for both artist and audience.

To reach this immersive state *with the presence of an audience*, the artist can be guided by the assumption that *an audience is in search of an immersive experience*. Rather than seeking merely to be entertained, people involve themselves in the arts to feel moved, to feel enhanced, to feel a part of the artistic experience. If we view the audience as needing to be entertained, we place ourselves in an external position where we need to perform for them or at them. This position not only decreases our own chances of being able to immerse in the artwork (the fear of being judged as inadequate or as a failure is too great) but also reduces the likelihood of audience participation. A natural human response to feeling force-fed is to resist. When the audience feels that the artist is just trying to entertain, they are likely to feel irritated and distanced by the effort.

Instead, a more helpful approach is for the artist to invite the audience into the immersive state. The artistic challenge is to draw the audience in. The artistic goal is to be swept away *with the audience*. Chances are, if the artist immerses in his art, the audience will follow along as long as their presence is kept in mind and factored in throughout the creative process. The performance is an attempt to communicate with the audience rather than to entertain them. The audience is drawn into the artist's space and the artist is drawn into the audience's space. This creates a mutual, shared experience that is gratifying for everyone.

The immersive experience of connecting with the audience can be even more powerful in a live performance or artistic show, when audience members share the experience with each other as well as with the artist. Recall the psychological experience of twinship, of being with like-kind. Members of an audience will influence each other's immersive potential by either energizing or deflating each other. The profound experience of being a part of an audience that is experiencing immersion is unforgettable and deeply enhances the overall experience of the art.

All in all, the kind of relationship an artist generates with his audience will affect his creative process. As with any kind of intimate relationship, the challenge involves finding an immersive connection while maintaining an independent sense of self. When this can be achieved, both the artist and the audience are gratified and fulfilled.

DEADLINES

Most artists have to deal with deadlines. Deadlines can be either a blessing or a curse. They can be perceived as an inhibiting pressure or as a useful container for the creative process. How an artist deals with deadlines depends on several factors.

One general consideration is how the artist experiences boundaries, particularly those imposed by others. An artist's reaction to deadlines often mimics his experience of his parents' attempts to control him during childhood. If he experienced his parents as controlling, he may have developed an automatic prototypical response of resistance. This is a natural human response and often operates outside of logic and reason. Most children will resist being controlled even when it is in their own best interests. ("You are not the boss of me!") When many of these kinds of encounters occur, the child develops a prototypical dance against external sources of control. ("When someone tries to control me, I resist. They increase their efforts at control, I resist more, and everyone gets angry.")

As adults, deadlines imposed by others can trigger this same automatic response. Deadlines can be felt as inhibiting forces that take away freedom and independence. They become something to resist and rebel against. ("Deadlines restrict my freedom of movement, and I resent that they are placed on me.") The artist may unconsciously resist these efforts to be controlled, even if it means that he suffers in the end. As in childhood, power struggles ensue between artist and agent, publisher, or producer.

The reality is that deadlines are a necessary part of artistic production. If an artist can examine his own history of preserving his sense of autonomy and independence, he can choose to change his reaction to these triggers.

Of course, the way that deadlines are presented can make a difference in the artist's response. If you feel that the deadline-imposer is unreasonable or insensitive to your process and struggles, you are likely to feel inhibited or even paralyzed by the deadline. Feeling alone and fearing failure, you are at risk of shutting down and falling into a vicious cycle of stress and nonproductiveness. If, however, you feel that the imposer appreciates your struggles and offers support (which may mean some measure of flexibility around the deadline), you will feel strengthened and bolstered, and this will support your productivity.

Generating your own deadlines can be a way to reduce resistance. If you can generate your own deadlines, you do not feel at risk of being controlled by an outside source. Self-determined deadlines can be experienced very differently from those that are imposed by others.

If you do not feel you have to fight against controlling others, you are more apt to view and use deadlines as helpful containers for your creative process. Deadlines can serve as comforting parameters for the free-floating anxiety and fear often experienced during the creative process. They can provide boundaries to the anticipation of never-ending anxiety.

Deadlines can also be experienced as incentives. Many artists describe how they need to break their project down into small, manageable chunks. Setting a series of deadlines for themselves, they can remain engaged in the project rather than feeling overwhelmed and paralyzed by its enormity. Setting bite-sized, consistent deadlines for various phases of your project also helps to moderate the fear of entry and immersion at any given point. Reaching for and meeting a series of small deadlines provides you with an ongoing sense of accomplishment. One writer I work with described breaking his project down into "day-tight compartments" so that he could feel accomplished at the end of each day's work. This process provides the confidence and strength that you need to follow the creative process through to completion of the project.

GUIDES

I. EXPLORE YOUR ASSUMPTIONS ABOUT YOUR AUDIENCE.

How do you fantasize about your audience? Are they hostile and critical? Appreciative and giving? Are they willing to follow you in your expression?

Make a reality check about the nature of your assumptions. Are these assumptions based on your past experience with an audience? Or are they based on your previous experiences in personal relationships?

For effective communication of your artistic message, your audience must be considered. View the audience as a potential new relationship. Your goal is to engage the audience in a two-way experience. Listen to them and reach out to them to invite them into your artistic space. Attempt to share your immersive experience *with them* rather than *presenting it to them*. This may involve considerable feelings of vulnerability, especially if you have negative assumptions about the audience's willingness to engage with you. Finding trust with an audience and becoming skillful at eliciting a relationship with them is perhaps one of your biggest challenges.

2. SET YOUR OWN DEADLINES.

Most artists have to deal with deadlines. Deadlines imposed by others can be experienced as insensitive pressures on your creative process — "I cannot be inspired on demand" or "The process unfolds in its own time." These statements are very true, and in a perfect world artists would not have to deal with the pressures of deadlines.

But in the real world, because responding to deadlines from others can trigger deep, self-preserving defenses against being controlled, it is usually best to develop your own deadlines. Even when dealing with externally imposed deadlines, you can retain your sense of control and autonomy by creating your own smaller deadlines within the allotted time frame. Making daily or weekly deadlines for yourself can keep you in charge of your project while still responding to the needs of your agent, publisher, producer, etc. Hold on to your own sense of your process, setting your own deadlines according to how you have come to know your needs.

You may also try to shift your perception of deadlines from restrictive efforts to control you to safe containers for your anxiety and your process. When a parent makes a rule not to play in the street, the rule is intended to protect the child from harm. The rule becomes a container for safety. If deadlines can be viewed as similar efforts to protect you from endless anxiety or from never completing your project, then they can be experienced as allies in your process.

3. BREAK YOUR PROJECT DOWN INTO SMALL CHUNKS.

It can be overwhelming and paralyzing to stand at the edge of a huge, overwhelming task. "Where do I begin?" "How will I ever do this?" Instead, imagine the project as consisting of a hundred smaller projects. The smaller the chunks you can organize, the better. Make the chunks bite-sized pieces: "Today I will decide what color to make the sky" or "Today I will draft an outline for the first section" or "Today I will compose the first three measures of the song."

This kind of organization will transform the larger project into a constant experience of movement and accomplishment. Creating smaller pools of water to immerse in also makes entry easier. ("I can't drown in a puddle.") By creating smaller scopes of engagement, the risk to your sense of safety is less than when trying to plunge into a huge, bottomless ocean.

Another way to break the project down is with time. Rather than expecting yourself to immerse for hours, set a time limit. "I will commit myself to the project for thirty minutes. If, at the end of thirty minutes, I still cannot immerse, I will consider it a day." Setting time limits is also another way to contain the anxiety around entry into immersion. It is easier to risk entry into creative immersion if you know that you will have to struggle for only thirty minutes, rather than for hours on end. If, after that time you still cannot find an immersive state, step back. Forcing yourself to keep trying will probably just escalate your frustration and anxiety. However, often you will find that once you make the commitment to attempt immersion, you will be able to dive in.

PART THREE

Stages of the Creative Process

(Charlie Kaufman, screenwriter [played by Nicholas Cage], sits at his typewriter with a blank page, struggling to begin his next screenplay and we hear his thoughts):

To begin, to begin . . . *(pause)* How to start . . . *(pause)* I'm hungry. I should get coffee . . . Coffee would help me think . . . But I should write something first . . . *(pause)* Then reward myself with coffee . . . Coffee and a muffin . . . Okay . . . *(pause)* . . . So I need to establish the themes . . . *(pause)* Maybe banana nut . . . That's a good muffin . . .

— FROM THE MOVIE *ADAPTATION*

CHAPTER EIGHT

Approaching Immersion

Wanderer, your footsteps are
The road, and nothing more;
Wanderer, there is no road,
The road is made by walking.
By walking one makes the road.

And upon glancing behind
One sees the path
That never will be trod again.
Wanderer, there is no road,
Only wakes upon the sea.

—— ANTONIO MACHADO,
"CAMINANTE / THE TRAVELER"

Rather than viewing the capacity to immerse as an all-or-nothing experience, we can understand it as consisting of several stages. Actual entry into the creative state is the result of successfully navigating these stages. Although I will describe them in a sequential, linear order, the completion of a work of art often involves moving back and forth between these stages countless times. The duration and intensity of each stage will vary depending on many factors. Some artists must go through each stage every time they approach the work. Others skip certain stages, having moved through them once. But generally, each phase is an important and natural part of the creative process.

The ability to immerse into a creative state varies for different people and at different times for the same person. At the one extreme is the artist who has no difficulty at all immersing into creation. As one of my clients, a visual artist, described it, "It is like breathing. I feel most comfortable, most at home when I am drawing. I don't believe there is a day that goes by that I don't draw. Drawing is my refuge." At the other end of the spectrum is the artist who wrestles with immersion. Another of my clients, a composer, is tortured by the prospect of immersion: "It is painful every step of the way. I struggle every single time I anticipate composing. I procrastinate, I delay, I allow myself distractions. It is the most difficult thing I try to do."

Although each of these artists describes different levels of ease in immersing into creativity, in our psychotherapy sessions it became clear that both moved through a series of internal and external stages toward creative activity. As I worked with each of them in individual therapy once a week, we became aware of the daily, even momentary, shifts in their internal experience and in the resulting impact on their capacity to immerse into creativity. For each, the capacity to immerse did not exist in a vacuum. We came to realize nuances and shifts in their internal and external sense of being-in-connection and how these fantasies and actual lived experiences affected their creative process.

Considerable anxiety and fear can be experienced at any point of transition between the stages of the process, from fantasy to contemplation to preparation. Moving into the next phase means moving into the unknown. And fear of this unknown can be paralyzing, blocking you from moving forward. Indeed, artists may stay indefinitely in any one of these stages. Anthony Storr compiled several such examples of the experience of the artist during this phase:

> Darwin's revolutionary idea of natural selection was incubating
> for at least twenty years before *On the Origin of Species by Means*

of Natural Selection was published, but he did not take long to write the book.... Brahms did not complete his first symphony until he was in his forty-third year. Yet he had made sketches for it, which he showed to Clara Schumann, as long as twenty years before this.... Beethoven's sketchbooks show how very often he was compelled to revise and rewrite his music.... Thackeray described himself as "sitting for hours before my paper, not doing my book, but incapable of doing anything else." ... Chopin is described by Georges Sand as "shutting himself up in his room for whole days, weeping, walking, breaking his pens, repeating and altering a bar a hundred times, spending six weeks on a single page."

The paralysis that many artists experience when trying to transition from stage to stage is often accompanied by negative feelings about themselves. Most feel that they should be able to do it by themselves or that they must do it by themselves. ("No one can do this for me.") Alone with this fear and anxiety, they assume their paralysis is due to their own weakness or defect. ("I'm a procrastinator" or "I am lazy" or "I don't have what it takes.") It is at these points of transition that we need the support of others to help us keep moving forward. Facing the fear of the unknown next phase requires the presence of a supportive other, whether in our real life or our fantasy life.

The previous chapters have laid the groundwork for understanding our basic need for relationships with mirrors, heroes, and twins. We can now use this framework to help us start and sustain our creative process through the completion of a project.

STAGE 1: FANTASY

The creative process is initially ignited through fantasies that draw on the types of relationships we have discussed: of greatness, of pleasing an admired other, and of feeling perfectly understood. These fantasies provide the fuel for creativity. They may be only vaguely conscious thoughts or they may be clear and vivid hopes and intentions. Whatever form these fantasies take, they provide the fertile psychological ground from which creativity grows.

At this initial stage, you may know what kind of artistic form you will use (dance, music, writing, etc.), but you will not have clarified a specific idea, feeling, or experience you wish to convey. Instead, this stage consists of imagining getting your fundamental needs for recognition, affirmation, and specialness met, which will then mobilize your energy toward the future project. Fantasies of being a famous artist can enhance your self-confidence — and you will need plenty of self-confidence and energy to engage in the risky prospect of immersion!

An opera singer I work with told me she was not aware of having such fantasies of greatness. "I just always knew that singing was what I wanted to do," she said. "I don't remember fantasies of greatness being the spark that started me on this path. I just knew." But on deeper reflection, she recalled being five or six years old and pretending to direct a make-believe choir. "I would be in my room for hours, with a record playing, and I pretended to be the conductor of a huge choir in front of a large audience. Now I remember that I would imagine getting standing ovations from the crowd. I decided at that point to pursue a singing career."

Fantasies of greatness and of a connection with powerful others are healthy psychological experiences that propel us forward. In fact, it can be argued that all creative processes are undertaken in an attempt to enhance or heal the self. When a person has not had adequate experiences of being recognized, affirmed, and applauded, creative projects can become a way to reach for these needed responses. Fundamentally, an artist hopes that his work (his self) will be seen, understood, and appreciated. Furthermore, for the artist who has experienced traumatic blows and disappointments to his feeling of specialness and safety (which occurs during abuse and/or neglect), creative acts can be an attempt to heal the self. The artist's hope for recognition and applause can ultimately be the hope to heal an injured or fragile self.

Artwork is often generated from pain and a feeling of aloneness. The need to express inner experience and to be heard by others is a powerful driving force behind creativity. In this way, the creative process is reflective of an artist's healthy longing for a sense of connectedness with others. Through artistic expression, the artist fantasizes sharing an immersive moment with others.

The creative process may also feel like the only safe kind of immersion for the artist. When other people have been unreliable or unavailable, the artist may turn to the creative endeavor as his sole source of immersive experience. Most likely, this artist has been affirmed as having a particular gift or talent, so he has come to trust artistic immersion as a safe place. However, he may feel that immersion with other people is completely unsafe and unreliable, so he isolates himself from others in his art. In this way, the artist reaches for connection with the artwork, an experience he has felt soothed or gratified by in the past. One writer, who had lost a significant relationship and who felt utterly alone in the world, described turning to his writing for comfort. "It is very soothing to express my pain in words... the words on the page are like a mirror of myself.... I can see myself there, make sense of myself there, find myself there."

Another fundamental fantasy that propels the desire to create is that of pleasing an admired figure. The fantasy may be to impress a parent, teacher, or other idol. This idolized figure may exist in reality or in fantasy; it doesn't really matter. But, like the small child who wants to be a grown-up or wants to please his parents, the artist can gain strength, inspiration, and vitality in this pursuit.

And the third driving force toward creativity can be the fantasy of being perfectly understood and appreciated. The artist expresses herself, her ideas, feelings, and perceptions, in hopes that others will resonate with the expression. The experience of belonging or feeling that she fits with others gives a powerful sense of enhancement. Although the fantasy may be that she will be understood and appreciated by everyone ("Never before has there been an artist who so completely won the hearts of all people . . ."), often a moderated form of this fantasy is sustaining enough. This hope for twinship can also make up for deficiencies in her real-life peer experiences.

In general, the creative process is ignited when the artist finds fantasies that supply hope for self-enhancement or self-cures. The hope to be heard and understood by an audience can exist alongside the hope of having something valuable to offer others. Imagining this mutual relationship with the audience can strengthen the artist toward the next stage in creativity. This is usually a time of enthusiastic anticipation for the artist. She has a vague notion about the artwork in the back of her mind but is not yet purposefully working toward giving it form or substance.

Many people never go beyond this stage in the creative process. These fantasies of greatness, acclaim, and stardom are often sustaining enough. Such a person may realistically assess that he does not have the skills or talent to actualize these fantasies. Or he may lack the supportive relationships that bolster his confidence to try. Without support and encouragement to engage in or develop his talents and skills, these fantasies may remain in the background. ("One day I'll . . .")

Allowing oneself to dream big is risky. Many people feel ashamed of these fantasies, viewing them as self-centered or immature. Others have been deflated or humiliated when they have dared to dream, being told that their dreams were unrealistic and unattainable. But if we can view these fantasies as fertile ground from which to grow, we can often rediscover our passions and creative energy. Reach out to mirrors, heroes, and twins that appreciate your dreams for support.

STAGE 2: CONTEMPLATION

When an artist experiences enough support for a particular artistic fantasy, he can proceed to the next phase toward immersion: contemplation. Here, his fantasies of greatness, of connecting with others through expression, and his hopes of pleasing an admired figure begin to be shaped into a usable art form. His hope of having his fantasies realized propels him toward action. These hopeful fantasies energize him and provide a feeling of purpose, meaning, and direction.

While he is still uncertain as to the specific art form that will emerge, he now begins to actively think about the project. What will be its content? What are the emotions and experiences he wishes to convey? As the artist thinks about the nature of the project, it takes on purpose and intent. He begins to experience a conscious awareness of his ideas, feelings, and images. He pays attention to his dreams and passing ideas. He starts to tune into the idea of the project: it is ever present in the back of his mind. Although it is not yet a focused effort, images begin to break through and flashes of form begin to emerge. These epiphanies of insight, organization, and clarity begin to build on each other. Often unwittingly, these ideas and images not only provide a foundation for the project but are also experienced by the artist as mini-immersive states that strengthen his sense of adequacy to the task. He will often record and store the content of these creative sparks for future use, although he may still be uncertain as to how they will be incorporated into the artwork. He begins to jot down notes, sketches, images, or ideas, energized by their presence and somewhat organized by their existence. But most important, the experience of these immersive flashes reassures the artist of his capacity for future, more total immersion.

Often, this phase of the creative process can feel like avoidance or procrastination. However, many artists I have worked with look back at this time and realize they needed this incubation period for ideas and images to emerge. Time was needed to sit with the initial stirrings of creative ideas, and often these stirrings occurred when they were not consciously focused on the project. Bertrand Russell describes an appreciation of this phase of the creative process:

> Very gradually I have discovered ways of writing with a minimum of worry and anxiety. When I was young each fresh piece of serious work used to seem to me for a time — perhaps a long time — to be beyond my powers. I would fret myself into a nervous state from fear that it was never going to come right. I would make one unsatisfactory attempt after another, and in the end have to discard them all. At last I found that such fumbling attempts were a waste of time. It appeared that after first contemplating a book on some subject, and after giving serious preliminary attention to it, I needed a period of subconscious incubation which could not be hurried and was if anything impeded by deliberate thinking. Sometimes I would find, after a time, that I had made a mistake, and that I could not write the book I had had in mind. But often I was more fortunate. Having, by a time of very intense concentration, planted the problem in my subconsciousness, it would germinate underground until, suddenly, the solution emerged with blinding clarity, so that it only remained to write down what had appeared as if in a revelation.

The phase of contemplation moves the artist from fantasy to reality through his commitment to the project. I recall this specific moment of transition in my process of writing this book. I was talking to my brother and told him my vague, still unorganized ideas about immersion and creativity and that I thought that I might have enough material for a book. His response helped me to transition into the contemplation stage: "That's great! Now, rather than saying that you're thinking about writing a book, say and know that you are writing a book. It already has a life, so give it a name right now." Initially, the thought of committing to the project felt premature. Was I emotionally ready to make such a statement? *Thinking about* writing a book felt much safer than *writing* a book. But the minute I declared to myself that I was writing a book, I realized that I had, indeed, already engaged in the process: "So I'm writing a book about creativity." This both energized and terrified me. But it moved me to concrete action.

STAGE 3: PREPARATION

At that moment, I entered into the next stage: preparation. "I am not at all prepared to make such a statement as 'I am writing a book,'" I thought. Where in the world would I begin? Research. Of course I needed to research. I needed to read everything anyone has ever written on creativity. After all, I began to think that my ideas probably held no merit or that they had been written about before. And I also felt that I needed to be an expert on creativity if I was to write a book about it. This is how I had always approached my academic writing: a literature review was crucial and I needed to be able to cite as many other experts as I could. "That's okay," I thought, "research. I'll be doing something productive toward my book and it is a safe, familiar place to start. No risk in research. Maybe I really can do this."

The research I did before starting to write helped me in several ways. I did end up incorporating much of the material into this book. More important, however, I believe doing the research served as a concrete ceremony and internal commitment, a kind of psychological gateway into devotion to the project. It also served as an experience of mirroring (I found that I really did have new ideas to add to the existing literature and this made me feel special and great), of idealization (I got to learn from other great thinkers), and twinship (I felt my experience and ideas were on a par with those of other writers on the subject).

The stage of preparation for immersion can be an attempt to

soothe the fear of the unknown. Preparation can take many forms, but typically it involves concrete actions and behaviors that are safe enough and function to keep the project alive on the horizon. Preparation serves as a way station in which to gather strength and confidence that will be needed to plunge into the immersive state. The artist's feeling of being prepared increases his sense of confidence (even if there is really no way to prepare for the unknown). It gives the artist an illusion of control that helps him take risks.

We can prepare ourselves for the immersive dive in a variety of ways. Research, as I was prompted to do, is one way to prepare. Another is to get the necessary tools that will be needed, such as a new costume or practice outfit for dance, a new computer, new art supplies, or a new instrument. These preparations give us the feeling of having something sturdy to hold on to when we eventually take the plunge.

Another method of preparing is to take care of other tasks extraneous to the project. Needing to make time for my creative activity, I will first clean the house, mow the yard, and shop for groceries. These tasks are really avoidance — after all, frightening things such as facing the unknown are usually best avoided — but they also may be another state of contemplation and serve to increase my sense of readiness to immerse into creativity. Since I don't really know what to expect when I sit down to write, I feel I must be prepared in case I have a major creative blitz — I wouldn't want to break it up by having to do the laundry! In other words, these preparations help to soothe my fear of creative immersion because they clear a path for its possibility, which internally gives me a feeling of being prepared for the dive.

Whether these preparatory activities lead to your immersion into creativity or are merely stalling tactics of procrastination, it is important to understand them as reflections of fear and not as indications of your weakness or inadequacy. Many artists come to me for therapy at this stage of their process, believing themselves to be defective, lazy, or weak. Reaching out for strengthening connections with others and with the artwork can help you move through these understandable fears.

Preparing for an artistic performance can involve a similar process. A singer I work with described a sequence of events that she always followed on the day of a performance. First, she slept late. When she woke up, she would have a leisurely breakfast. Then she would run through all of her music for the show in her mind, performing it in her imagination. Then she would take a nap. After the nap, she would then get dressed and feel ready for the show.

She said that she understood this entire preparation as a way to conserve her energy for the performance. Because immersion in performing is so intense, she felt she could not spare an ounce of energy before the show. In fact, she also needed her space from others the entire day of the show. She could not tend to any needs of her husband or children because she felt it would drain too much of her energy. If her sequence was interrupted, she anticipated the performance with much more anxiety.

We came to understand how her need for space and detachment from others during her preparation was actually formed in childhood. As we discussed her history, she described how her mother had been emotionally unavailable to her throughout her life. She felt that her mother had nothing to give her and guarded her own personal space from her children very carefully. Her mother was not physically affectionate or emotionally supportive. This singer was struck with how much she reminded herself of her mother when she was in this preparatory phase before a performance. We both wondered if her need for complete distance from others during this time was a defensive reaction to her fear of the anticipated immersion. She knew that immersion in her performance required a complete investment of her energy. She feared that her family would drain her if she did not put up a solid wall around herself. This was also the way that she had understood her mother's distance: "We kids needed more than our mother had to offer." Her fundamental relationship prototype of being with others was that people were a drain; other people did not provide support and energy. Instead, relating with others meant putting out but getting nothing in return. As a child she learned to fend for herself and to deal with anxieties and fears on her own. It made sense that she would use the same coping strategy in her anticipations of her performances.

Once she recognized how she felt she needed to shield herself from others in order to sustain her energy, she could consciously determine if this was still true with her husband and children. Would they be merely a drain on her, or could they actually offer her support and strength? Although she continued to isolate herself on the day of a performance, she was able to slowly risk a new pattern by asking her husband to give her backrubs on the day of a show. She found he was more than happy to help her relax, and this small change served as a shift in all her assumptions about what others might be able to offer her.

The preparation phase also consists of self-evaluation and comparison to others. The artist may run his beginning inclinations of the project past others to get their response. He needs to know if it has merit and whether his anticipated immersion into the project is worth the risk. The artist can begin to question and doubt his own perceptions and the reality of his fantasies of specialness. His fear of humiliation, of falsely believing himself to be special with something to offer, can propel this need for a reality check with peers and mentors.

An additional fear can also surface: he dreads to repeat previous disappointments with others. "Maybe no one will care" and "Maybe everyone will dislike my work" are fears that may reflect his previous injuries and rejections. They arise from his earlier lived experiences of hearing messages such as "What you say and feel doesn't matter" or "What you are expressing is wrong or invalid." He is putting himself at considerable risk of getting these same painful responses by displaying himself in the current project. However, it is better now, at this stage of the process (when he is still somewhat self-protected) to put himself out there for evaluation, rather than after he has taken the plunge and has let down all of his protective shields.

At this point of evaluation by self and others, an artist may be confronted with deficits, or holes, in his talent or skills. Trying to prepare as fully as he can for his anticipated dive, the artist may decide he needs a refresher course in the basics of his trade or feel that he needs certain refinements to his technical skills. Many artists will periodically take an introductory-level class in their art form in order to stay grounded in fundamental technique. This can give the artist the courage to later break some rules or to travel into new and evolved forms far beyond basic technique.

In addition, since creativity often involves integrating and playing with previously unassociated realms or topics, the artist may need to acquire knowledge and skills that are outside of her typical medium of expression. The novelist who wants to write historical fiction may have a great deal of research to do about a period in history. The classical musician who conceives a new genre of style through the integration of jazz or rock may need to learn new techniques and instruments. Any particular project can require learning new skills or knowledge in another realm, and the artist engages in this learning in an effort to feel and be more prepared for his ultimate immersive experience.

Another important part of the preparation period may be for the artist to immerse herself in other realms. Particularly when she is feeling vulnerable and fragile (as a consequence of the self-evaluation experience), she may need to find strength through immersing in spirituality, intimate relationships, art appreciation, or psychotherapy. Stepping away from her own project and allowing herself to connect with her husband or to be swept away by the beauty and intensity of another piece of art or to be completely understood and appreciated by her therapist can restrengthen her and give her the hope and confidence she needs to immerse in her artwork. This movement between immersive realms is a critical component of sustaining the creative process because it can enhance and bolster an artist's resilience to the fears she confronts along the way.

Throughout this stage, rudimentary ideas and images of the project continue to germinate, evolve, and develop. (Recall Bertrand Russell's insight and the ultimate achievements of artists described by Anthony Storr.) These pockets of creative sparks are supported within these preparatory activities and within immersion in other realms and connections. Support from others is crucial to moving through this stage. Because we are close to the edge, preparing ourselves for the immersive dive, we are excited but fearful. Reaching out for the three kinds of support from others (a reflection of our greatness, being taken under the wing of an admired person, and belonging to a group of like-kind) strengthens us so we can see where these creative flashes will lead.

GUIDES

1. IDENTIFY YOUR CURRENT PHASE IN THE CREATIVE PROCESS.

Are you in the fantasy, contemplation, or preparation phase? Each phase is necessary and productive. Each phase may last varying amounts of time. You may move forward and backward among the phases, and you may experience more than one phase simultaneously.

Evaluate the usefulness of your efforts during each phase. Do you need additional support or training to feel the strength to move to the next phase? If you do, put your energy into that. It is not avoidance or distraction. It is serving to bolster your confidence and skill to take that eventual dive.

Transitioning between phases can be frightening. Identify and validate the nature of your fears at each transition point. When you do this, you will begin to see your own unique patterns and tendencies in coping with these fears. The development of rituals (I always make flavored coffee before I sit down to write) and structures (scheduling blocks of time) can help with transitions and with moving beyond the fear.

2. TURN TO OTHERS FOR SUPPORT.

Eliciting support from others is probably the most important thing you can do to help with transitioning among the phases. You do not have to do this alone. In fact, you probably can't do this alone. If you do not have an appreciative, encouraging support network, developing one will be an important part of your overall process. But in the absence of current, real-life support, try to draw on memories of previously supportive others or fantasize about a future appreciative audience. Fantasizing about the appreciation of an idol or other mentor can be especially strengthening. Whether in reality or fantasy, the experience and anticipation of being appreciated and applauded can give a person the courage to proceed toward immersion.

CHAPTER NINE

Diving In

It begins as an unknown adventure in an unknown space. It is at the moment of completion that in a flash of recognition they are seen to have the quantity and function which was intended. Ideas and plans that existed in the mind at the start were simply the doorway through which one left the world in which they occurred.

— MARK ROTHKO

I am seeking, I am striving, I am in it with all my heart.

— VINCENT VAN GOGH

You have successfully navigated the first three stages of the creative process: fantasy, contemplation, and preparation. You feel as ready as you will ever be to immerse into your project. You are ready to dive in.

STAGE 4: TAKING THE PLUNGE

No matter how much you have fantasized about success, contemplated your contribution, and prepared for your project, you come to the point where you must sit with an empty slate and begin your creation. Simultaneously, you feel that you have prepared enough and that you have no preparation for this moment at all. Even though you may have notebooks full of research, a compilation of nuggets of ideas and images, and even, perhaps, a carefully outlined map of your project, you are now at that hopeful yet terrifying edge of immersing into creativity itself. To do this, you must freefall into the project, allowing your ideas and images to guide you to the next movement and rhythm. You begin to feel that the art form has a mind, a soul of its own, and your job is to listen to its voice and surrender to its form.

I will never cease to be amazed that no matter how much I "think about" writing my next section or chapter, the ideas and the flow of form and content evolve out of the writing process itself. Part of my preparation for writing is first to gather bits of thoughts and then to develop a rather detailed outline. Although these efforts are by no means useless (I usually make use of the outline and incorporate many of the ideas), the process of writing breathes its own life into the words. New ideas and associations are presented to me through the process. Clarity of form evolves as I go. Thoughts and feelings come up that never would have occurred to me in my contemplative and preparatory phases, no matter in how much detail or how thoroughly I had thought about it. When I am writing, I am "in the book," as much a spectator and observer of the material as a creator of it.

Out of immersion with the artwork comes creativity. Joan Miró said, "The painting rises from the brushstrokes as a poem rises from the words. The meaning comes later." Engaging in connection with the art form propels it toward actualization. The sculptor R. A. Baillie described his experience:

> As your carving progresses, the stone itself will suggest improvements over your first sketch. If you are sensitive to its messages, you will modify certain details as you work — leaving a

bold plane where your sketch indicated a round or broken surface. . . . Many stones have veins, much as wood has a grain, and
sometimes by following what these veins suggest you will get a
finer effect than you had ever thought of when you were making your clay model.

This process never fails to surprise and delight me. I suppose that
after facing the entry point time after time, I have come to rely on
this magic. But even as I write that, I am reminded of the anxious
feeling, even close to panic, that I still experience as I anticipate a
writing session. I suppose that in these moments, I still doubt and fear
that it will not work this time, that the book will be silent and I will
face the blank page alone.

This anxiety and fear have led me to develop certain rituals
to help me enter into the immersive state. These are silly, meaningless rituals, but somehow executing them helps me to muster my
courage to face the challenge. First, I have found that writing in the
morning is much easier for me than writing later in the day. I understand this as a form of "not thinking too much about it." If I delay
writing until later in the day, as I often do when I have morning
appointments or am feeling the need to prepare by doing other chores
first, I find that my anxiety about writing increases throughout the
day. Usually by lunchtime I am too stressed by the idea and give up
for the day. This pattern can extend for days, even weeks at a time,
and it will often feel like I will never be able to reenter the creative
state.

One thing that helps me to sit down to write in the morning is to
make a cup of flavored coffee. Not just regular coffee — it must be
cinnamon, vanilla, or hazelnut. Maybe it is the sense of giving myself
a treat since I am going to do this anxiety-provoking thing. Or maybe
it's having something warm to hold on to that soothes me. However
it has worked for me, flavored coffee is now associated with productive work, so I always make it.

Another ritual for me is to handwrite my initial draft. Somehow it feels more intimate, that I am in closer connection with the ideas as they are initially presented to me. I am too old to have grown up with computers, so perhaps typing at a computer still feels grafted on for me. After I get a handwritten draft of the initial ideas, then I can type it in the computer and start revisions. But working with pen and paper initially helps me to feel physically connected with the words. Much slower — but more connected.

Other artists have described to me the rituals they have developed to help them with the point of entry. They are often objects or sequences of actions that help them to feel courageous and connected. A painter reported always putting on a certain pair of wool socks before painting (even in the summer!). A composer told me that she would go through a series of checks before sitting down at the piano (checks her email, checks her voicemail, . . .). And a choreographer described a particular series of stretches — she called them her creative stretches — she would do before creating a dance. Psychologically, the structure that rituals provide can be a strengthening influence. Especially during times of change or stress, structure serves as a container that helps a person feel safe and protected.

THE IMMERSIVE STATE

The immersive state, where creativity and hope are generated, can last a few minutes to a few days or even weeks. Because it involves a relationship with the art form, it is like any other intimate relationship that ebbs and flows in the experience of synchronicity. Sometimes, an artist has an easy, immediate connection with the art, as if there is no getting-acquainted period necessary. The great German poet and dramatist Goethe said, "The songs made me, not I them; the songs had me in their power." As Thackeray described writing his novels, "It seems as if an occult Power was moving the pen." And Thomas

Wolfe, author of *Look Homeward, Angel* stated, "I cannot really say the book was written. It was something that took hold of me and possessed me."

A composer I see for psychotherapy described how some songs seem to fall into his lap. The song is nearly complete when it presents itself to him. It is an effortless experience, almost as if his only task is to transcribe the music onto the page. When this experience occurs, he can sustain immersion for hours and days, ending only when the song is fully complete. He comes out (out of his studio and out of the immersive state) with a finished product that clearly had its own beginning and end.

There are many other artists who, once they have immersed themselves into the project after varying amounts of time spent in pre-immersive states of fantasy, contemplation, and preparation, find they are able to complete a work with relative ease and speed. Robert Louis Stevenson wrote *Treasure Island* at the rate of a chapter a day for sixteen chapters; Mozart composed his three last and greatest symphonies within six weeks.

At other times, however, an artist experiences immersion only in brief spurts. The composer-client I mentioned above described a very different experience with other songs. "I feel tortured the entire time. It took me years to write this one song. It would only come to me one small piece at a time." He described the experience of composing the song as piecing together a thousand brief immersive moments. Because it involved a process of rapid cycling in and out of immersive states, he had to deal with the anxiety of reentry over and over. "It was hell," he said.

Even the most gifted of artists can experience difficulties connecting with certain projects that end up being great works of art. One example is William Blake in writing his well-known poem "The Tiger." This fairly short poem is distinguished for its extraordinary intensity and unity. But the various drafts of the poem reveal the complicated process the poet went through, suggesting and rejecting numerous ideas until he decided on the final version. Similarly, Samuel Taylor Coleridge said of writing "Christabel" that "Every line has been produced by me with labor-pangs." And the contemporary poet Stephen Spender says, "I dread writing poetry[;] ... a poem is a terrible journey, a painful effort of concentrating the imagination."

Thus, as in relationships with other people, the artist can have a sense of the artwork as being easily known or as hard to get to know. The artwork itself can exist on a continuum as apparent or disguised. And depending on the nature of the artwork, the artist can have varied experiences of self-identity and self-confidence. (Recall that your sense of yourself is largely defined in the context of relationships: with some people you feel strong and with others you feel weak; with some you feel confident and with others you feel insecure.) In effect, different pieces of work can make us feel more or less competent, confident, and connected.

The relationship we have with a particular piece of work can affect the quality of our immersive experience. In the case when the composer was easily immersed with the song as it presented itself to him, he described the oceanic bliss experience of being so easily and totally engaged with the music that he felt strong, powerful, and vitalized. Immersion was an effortless state. He felt as one with the song and merged with its beauty and fluidity. Here, the song was his friend, an ally. He could not, nor did he want to, separate or disengage from it. He stayed merged until it was complete.

This is the kind of immersive experience we all long for. It is a feeling of cohesion and organization within us where everything comes together. It is an experience of healing and enhancement. It is a sense of grace through expression, a feeling of conveying the deepest parts of ourselves adequately, perfectly, and beautifully. In this state, we do not even consider evaluation by others. We are fully engaged and reflected in the intimate connection with the art form.

We lose a sense of our self and a sense of time. We feel, at once, that we are playing with our most inner and unique sense of self and that we are being deeply affected and redefined each moment by the soul of the artwork.

This immersion of every part of our self into the artwork feels, simultaneously, like we are losing our old self and discovering a new self. The connection with the art form touches each of our senses, and in playing with the art, we are being created as much as we are creating. We know deep down that this experience of immersion will transform us: we hope the engagement enhances us, but we also fear it could demolish us.

Picasso once said, "A picture used to be a sum of additions. In my case it is a sum of destructions. I do a picture — then I destroy it. In the end, though, nothing is lost: the red I took away from one place turns up somewhere else. . . . The destroying transforms it, condenses it, makes it more substantial." This process of destruction-creation applies to our experience of ourselves during artistic immersion as well: we must temporarily lose our self — give up our previously held notions of control and independence — in order to create an intimate relationship with the artwork. It can be a frightening edge of the self: Will I be able to connect with the artwork? Will I be able to sustain my sense of self? Can I trust that something new and meaningful will evolve? Or will my efforts be met with only emptiness and frustration?

Children can immerse into creativity and play much more easily than adults because they haven't yet experienced as many painful rejections and disappointments, so they have less of a need to control. Picasso understood this when he said, "Every child is an artist. The problem is how to remain an artist once he grows up." If we remind ourselves to approach immersion with a sense of play, we can open ourselves to the connection, the expression, and the passion of creative engagement.

Immersing one's self in the mutual play with the art form propels both artist and art form forward. As D. W. Winnicott described this mutual exchange, "It is in playing and only in playing that the individual child or adult is able to be creative and to use the whole personality, and it is only in being creative that the individual discovers the self."

There are artists who do not even display their work to others. They engage in creative acts for this experience alone. Because it is so internally satisfying and enhancing, they have no need for applause, or they fear that the experience would be ruined if they got a negative response. This artist is not intending to share her work with others. She is engaging in creativity for the immersive experience itself, and she keeps her artistic play private, for her own use.

Unfortunately, this easy and effortless connection with a work of art is not always experienced. As in the example of the composer who was tortured all through the composition, sometimes we can experience the artwork as an adversary, hard to get to know, hard to get hold of. We must struggle with self-preserving defenses in this relationship. This kind of creative experience is constantly broken apart, and we can feel personally broken apart in the process. It is an intense love-hate relationship, where we feel by turns adequate and inadequate. This kind of relationship is filled with confusion, self-doubt, and fear. We move in and out of immersive states, sometimes retreating from the project altogether out of despair and hopelessness. Chapter 10 will address this type of painful disengagement and will offer ideas about moving through it.

CRAFTING

A special type of immersive state is crafting. Crafting is the rehearsals, the rewrites, the revisions. It is the creative work with directors, with editors, with collaborators, with the audience. Crafting requires focus and intent. I imagine crafting as a position between deep immersion and disengagement. The crafting phase in the creative process is when the artist steps back from his flurry of new ideas and turns instead to refining the form of his raw creation. Crafting involves a cognitive element of experience, where the artist examines the creation and begins to integrate and define its boundaries and parameters. It is a problem-solving process: how to perfect, join together, or add technical proficiency to the form and content. Skill and technique are primarily engaged. External requirements are closely examined and considered. The raw artistic work is cleaned up. The details of the creative expression are defined and developed. The artist sustains immersion in creativity as he keeps an evaluative eye on his work.

An artist can have wide, often rapid fluctuations in his feelings of competence, safety, and value during crafting. One moment he may experience his work as brilliant, and the next he may feel that it has no value whatsoever. An artist may shift from feeling extremely hopeful and strengthened to being overwhelmed and despairing.

Crafting is an intense phase of creativity that requires persistence and patience. The artist has a heightened need for supportive others during this time. With this support, the artist is strengthened to reengage with the work. And the artwork is ultimately moved from raw self-expression to an intricate and purposeful piece of art.

After periods of creative immersion, we will naturally disengage from the artwork. As we step back from our connection with the artwork, we can feel deeply gratified and enhanced, or acutely threatened and vulnerable. How we cope with these periods of disengagement will affect our future capacities to immerse, so I will now turn to this final phase of the creative process.

GUIDE

PLAY, PLAY, PLAY!

Immerse into the connection with the artwork and allow yourself to play in the moment, play with the artistic medium, and feel the soul of the artwork. Approach immersion with a sense of playful curiosity about what will evolve. Reinterpret your racing heartbeat and shortness of breath as excitement rather than fear. Focus on immersing into the connection with the artwork rather than trying to control it. And remember, no one can stay immersed all the time. (This would, in fact, be an indication of severe pathology.)

CHAPTER TEN

Coping with Disengagement and Reentry

Most writers enjoy only two brief periods of happiness. First, when what seems like a glorious idea comes flashing to mind, and secondly, when a last page has been written and you have not had time yet to consider how much better it all ought to have been.

— J. B. PRIESTLY

I can go months, sometimes even years, without writing a solitary word.

— DAVID MARKSON

At some point, the wholeness of the immersive state is broken apart. We disengage from the intense fusion with the artwork and come back to our-selves-as-separate-from-the-artwork, although we now also return to a "new self" that has evolved in the process. This movement out of immersion is a normal and natural part of the creative process. It is a worthwhile phase of creativity in which we stand back from our work, evaluating it from the outside and making tweaks and adjustments as we deem necessary.

Disengagement can be a positive or negative experience in the creative process. It is a time when we can rest, feel enhanced by our productivity, and be proud of our work-in-progress. However, it is also a time when we are vulnerable to the darkness: depression, anxiety, and other negative psychological consequences. How we cope with disengagement from the creative process will determine the fluidity and ease of our eventual reentry into immersion.

UNDERSTANDING THE CAUSES OF DISENGAGEMENT

Many different factors can cause disengagement. I will outline them here to help you make sense of your own breaks.

External Interruptions

The first kind of immersive break results from the demands of time or your schedule. When life or other demands on your time intervene, you will be forced to put an artificial end to your immersive connection with the project. Often, this is experienced as quite frustrating, as you may feel that if you were without these interruptions, you would naturally sustain your immersive state. A composer told me that she felt most supported by her husband when he took over household and child-care chores when she was in a creative state. His taking on these duties allowed her to sustain her creativity based solely on her internal experience.

A well-known story about the poet Samuel Taylor Coleridge offers a rather extreme example of how susceptible the delicate creative state is to outside intrusions. Coleridge described how he wrote "Xanadu: The Ballad of Kubla Khan" in a note attached to the poem: the poem, he said, had "presented itself" to him in an opiate dream. When he awoke, his task was merely to dictate the poem onto paper. Partway through his transcription, someone knocked on his door. He answered it but then found that he had forgotten the rest of the piece. His immersive connection with the poem was broken and he could not reenter that space. Knowing how delicate immersion can be, we can take steps to insulate ourselves from interruptions.

Running Out of Energy

Another break in immersion can happen when you run out of energy. Although the intensity of immersive connection is energizing and vitalizing, it is also emotionally and physically tiring. When you experience a creative flurry of connection with the artwork, often you will sustain this immersive state for hours (sometimes even days). Unaware of the passage of time and not tending to your physical needs, you may work to the point of exhaustion. When your physical and psychic energy eventually run out, you are forced to disengage to sleep and eat.

At some level, you may drive yourself to this point of exhaustion out of a fear that you will be unable to reenter the immersive state if you let go of it. I have worked with several artists who always stop for the day at a point where they are clear about the next step. Leaving the artistic engagement with clarity about what is to come next makes reentry much easier for them than if they disengage at a point of frustration. This way, the next period of immersion is anticipated with a clear starting point rather than apprehension about emptiness or the need for problem solving.

Problems or Stumbling Blocks

Disengagement can also occur when you hit a stumbling block in the artistic process. The harmonious experience of dancing along perfectly with the artwork is disrupted when something doesn't work or when you run into a problem or glitch. What was once a fluid, effortless relationship can now be experienced as frustrating and adversarial. You can feel that the artwork is no longer a perfect reflection or a perfect mirror of your talent. You may disengage from the project out of a need for self-preservation.

This type of disengagement occurs when you need to regain your feeling of adequacy and control. It is a defensive disengagement, as you fear that your underlying feelings of inadequacy will be confirmed if you keep struggling with the project. You may fear being annihilated by the project: that the artwork is beating you or that you are not good enough to complete the work. This disruption in the harmonious flow between you and your artwork can point out that you are, indeed, separate from the artwork, and this can raise your insecurities and doubts about your performance.

Out of this fractured self-confidence, you may totally reject the project ("It wasn't a good idea anyway"), or you may devalue yourself ("I just don't have what it takes to do this"). If you do not have alternative realms of support (such as other relationships, spirituality, etc.), you may be at risk of abandoning the project or even your identity as an artist.

For example, one novelist I worked with wrote the first thirty pages of her story without a hitch:

> I was in a flow of introducing characters and their relationships with each other, while the story line was continuing to evolve in the back of my mind. I wasn't consciously mapping out the chapters. I just knew that my involvement in the process was leading me to places I needed to go. But then it struck me: these two characters would never interact the way that I was portraying them. I was completely ignoring certain facets of their personalities. And then, wait, if they had a different relationship, that would make the entire story go in a different direction. All of a sudden, I was confused and disorganized. What had I done? Maybe the entire story needed to be different. What direction was I heading? Out of my frustration, I felt like ripping up the whole thing. But I didn't feel like I could start all over. I couldn't tell what was good about it, where it went wrong, or what I could do to fix it. I was totally deflated. At that moment,

I wanted to scrap the entire project — no, my entire career as an author. This was just too hard. What was once a source of energy and pride for me turned into my nemesis. I couldn't imagine reorganizing the whole thing. It felt too overwhelming. I couldn't trust that I had the talent or intellect to sort it out. I turned off my computer, walked away and got depressed. I haven't gone back to it since.

Emotionally Threatening Artistic Content

Another kick-out from immersion is when the content of the artistic expression becomes too threatening. I have witnessed this with people in psychotherapy: we had been able to create a safe space together, a space where it was okay to reveal feelings and parts of themselves they had kept hidden for years. Within this safe relationship, they began to express and experience their longings, fears, hopes, and dreads. Often, these emotional experiences had been locked up for so long the person was surprised by their presence and intensity. Feeling and expressing such pain and longing was frightening. "I didn't realize how much that had hurt me" and "I'm afraid that I'll never stop crying" are common reactions to this felt freedom to express. They feared that their emotions would drown them or that they would be humiliated in their "raw nakedness"; this often caused them to retreat emotionally back into their shell.

Creating art can involve a similar process and can raise similar fears. As an artist totally invests himself in a work of art, the product is often an expression of deep emotions and experience. Often, an artist may not even be consciously aware of some aspects of himself. When they are expressed in his artwork, he may feel surprised, frightened, or exposed. He may need to disengage from the artwork out of a fear of being engulfed by his emotions, a fear of humiliation in his state of exposure, or a need to integrate this "new information." He may need to rework his sense of identity by separating from the artwork in order to reengage with the art later from a more organized core.

This initially disorganizing experience of deepened self-awareness through artistic expression can be a profound one. It is one way that immersion generates transformation and growth. But the break-through of previously repressed or avoided emotional experiences can be disturbing and even frightening. When we get shifted around internally, we feel disorganized, split up, and quite vulnerable. It is risky for the artist to go there. But it also is what makes for compelling works of art, because the reflection of this internal depth is evident and touches the audience at the core.

Waiting

The process of creativity often involves waiting for feedback from others. Whether this wait entails a few seconds (for an immediate response from an audience) or a few months (for an evaluation of work submitted to an agent or editor), it leaves the artist in a vulnerable state.

One of my clients, a composer, described her vulnerabilities during this time:

> Waiting is brutal. I feel like my entire self is on the line. My work will be good enough or it won't. I'll be good enough or I won't. I swing back and forth from feeling confident and hopeful to dreading the rejection that I'm certain is coming. At times, I feel high on the anticipation of being affirmed as gifted, talented, and wonderful. At other times, I feel that I am just waiting to be annihilated, that all my dreams of success were merely an illusion. Like I'll feel humiliated: who was I to think that my work is valuable? It was all a fantasy. It's an emotional roller coaster ride. It's stressful and exhausting. And, oh yeah, I get totally paralyzed when I'm waiting. I can't work. I need feedback before I can work again. Never do I feel so helpless, so powerless, and so vulnerable, as when I'm waiting.

Support from others is critical during this time. But we can feel so fragile that we fear even the slightest disappointment from others. This fear can lead us to withdraw from others at a time when we need to reach out to them even more.

The Feeling of Overexposure

The sudden feeling of overexposure, or the realization that you have opened and revealed your most core self to others in your art, can also halt an immersive state. This can happen when you look up from your artistic connection and suddenly realize how emotionally naked you are *in front of others*. Your self-protective shields have been down, and you become aware that you have displayed your inner life in the project. This sudden awareness of self-exposure can lead to a feeling similar to panic: with nowhere to run, nowhere to hide, you may feel helpless to protect yourself from a suddenly evident audience.

Your past experiences with audiences are likely to color your reaction at this awareness of exposure. If you have experienced prior audiences as hostile or critical, you are likely to feel the threat of repeated humiliation, ridicule, or embarrassment in this state of openness. (When I use the term *audience*, I mean both personal and artistic responses from others.) Prior negative reactions can be reflexively felt in this state of vulnerability, almost like the brain setting off flashing warning signals of anticipated danger. Your feelings of vulnerability and overexposure are often reflected in dreams of being naked in an inappropriate social setting. Naked and exposed, you respond automatically by covering up and, in effect, withdrawing from the immersive experience.

Criticism

And finally, another rupture to immersive connection can be actual negative feedback from another person. Once an artist is able to enter into the immersive state, she lets go of her own observing eye that would monitor her work from an external position. In fact, she is not feeling in charge of the flow of creation at all; she is merely in it, partly consumed by it and partly consuming it. As I have described earlier, the immersive state allows the experience of pure freedom and hope within connection. It is a state of total fusion with the art and one that is free of psychologically protective shields and barriers. Because it allows for such freedom of expression, the artist is able to float around in her imagination from primitive to complex parts of her being. The experience of pure perfection of the self, of the other (the artwork), and of the process itself can exist in this place of total connection.

Now imagine that this state of perfection is interrupted by a critical other: "That color doesn't really work there, does it?" The artist's experience of perfect union is broken apart. She must step outside of the immersive space to evaluate the criticism: "Is that true? Is there something wrong with what I've done?"

When criticism or negative feedback intrudes on an artist's immersive experience, not only is the perfect union dismembered, but the artist's sense of self can also be fragmented. Especially when the artist already feels fragile and vulnerable, criticism during the immersive experience can be especially damaging. The artist may swing to the self-protective extreme position of doubting the entire work ("Maybe this whole thing is shit") or doubting himself ("Maybe I can't judge what is good") or losing trust in his own competency ("I'm just a fraud"). When criticism assaults an artist in this position of openness and vulnerability, not only is the immersive connection broken apart, but he can also experience the criticism as an attack on his personal identity. The ultimate danger is that artistic immersion will no longer be considered a safe and trustworthy place.

MOVING THROUGH DISENGAGEMENT

Although immersive experience can be interfered with, or even broken apart, in a number of ways, the resulting experience is one of disengagement. As I have said, this can be a positive or a negative psychological experience. Most commonly, it is a time of wide fluctuations in feelings about one's self and the project. One minute an artist can feel convinced of the brilliance of the work, and the next she can feel certain that the work has no value whatsoever. The nature of our experience during disengagement, and our ultimate ability to reengage with our work, depends on several factors: (1) an understanding of how the immersive connection was lost; (2) the availability of empathic others; (3) the availability of alternative realms of immersion; (4) the underlying strength and resilience of the artist's psychological self; and (5) the capacity for acceptance and letting it be.

Understanding How the Immersive Connection Was Lost

When immersive connection is lost because of time or energy constraints rather than as a result of some emotional threat or danger (criticism, emotional awareness, or overexposure), the artist can typically leave the immersive experience feeling strengthened and enhanced. As I suggested before, it can be helpful to stop at a point of knowing what you want to do next so anticipation of reentry feels easier, more known. And if you are in a period of waiting for feedback, remind yourself that this is an understandably difficult period for any artist (your anxiety makes sense) and try to immerse yourself in other realms and connections.

But even when the artist's safety and trust in artistic immersion are not fractured, he may still experience an empty depression between immersive encounters. He may be left feeling somewhat lost or afloat, flat or at a loss. As with someone missing a lover, life goes on but it lacks the energy and fulfillment experienced when they were together. Most artists in this space continue to work on the project in their minds, coming up with new ideas or mapping out the next stroke. Such ongoing internal connection with the art serves to bolster confidence and readiness to reenter an immersive state. The artist continues to look forward to the next immersive experience once time permits or once she is rested.

The experience of a problem or glitch with the project itself may leave the artist feeling deflated and insecure. Although the safety of his entire self may not feel at risk, he may be plagued by insecurities about the project during disengagement. If he doubts his capacities to solve the problem, he may avoid reentry into immersion and may need to progress through the phases of fantasy, contemplation, and preparation once again before feeling ready to resume work on the project.

The artist who suffers a more emotionally painful immersive break may also have a more difficult experience during disengagement. In these instances, where the artist feels threatened by humiliation, overexposure, or inadequacy, he walks away from the immersive experience feeling injured, threatened, scared, and defensive. If the immersive rupture was particularly acute, he may feel that his entire psychological stability is at risk.

In this more painful state of disengagement, the artist may feel depressed and anxious. When his artistic expression involves the revelation of deeply rooted emotional pain and conflict, he may be left with a new awareness of feelings and memories he had previously split off. He may dread to repeat previous injuries and disappointments ("I couldn't stand to be humiliated again"), so he withdraws from the project to protect himself.

I once worked with a poet who experienced this kind of intensive disengagement. Actually, she had stopped writing poetry for a number of years. She entered psychotherapy with symptoms of depression, anxiety, nightmares, and a lack of memory of her childhood before the age of thirteen. She recalled being physically abused by her father as a teenager and being neglected by her mother. She and I created a safe space within the psychotherapy sessions. After two years of treatment, many of her symptoms had subsided, and she had begun to feel an increased energy and vitality for life. She spontaneously began writing poems again, bringing each one to show me. We both celebrated her return to writing; aside from being gifted again with words, she also felt that she was recapturing a part of herself and a part of her lifelong coping style.

But one day she appeared for our session in tears. She was disorganized; she had trouble speaking in sequential sentences and was beside herself with anxiety. She handed me her latest poem. I read it right there — she seemed to need to communicate something to me that she couldn't verbalize. My heart froze as I read her poem, depicting actual sexual abuse by her father. There, on the paper, was a painful account of a little girl being raped, staring at the patterns in the wallpaper in an effort to distance herself from what was being done to her. The poem was not complete. It was apparent that she had abruptly stopped writing due to the traumatic experience of recalling the abuse.

Before writing this poem, she had walled off the memory and the associated feelings of the molestation. Through the safety she had experienced, first in psychotherapy and then in her poetic expression, she was able to reconnect with this memory. Although it was initially devastating to her, she also experienced it as necessary and productive to her overall mental health. But she stopped writing poetry again, this time fearful of the revelation of more memories and being overwhelmed by the pain.

She needed, instead, to turn back to our relationship for strength. Through my understanding of her experience, she was able to reorganize and re-create her sense of self, this time integrating the memory of her past and the accompanying feelings and meanings the traumas carried.

It is interesting to note that this woman did, indeed, reconstitute her sense of self and reorganized into a stronger person. She was able to use her writing talent toward her further healing and her ongoing efforts to deal with her traumatic past. She became an advocate for abused and neglected children. She also began to write children's books, specifically dealing with girls' self-perceptions and body images.

This example illustrates how the creative process can generate transformative experience for the artist. However, at times it can also bring up feelings, memories, and meanings that had previously been buried for self-preservation. When this occurs, the presence of another immersive relationship (in this case, our psychotherapeutic relationship) may be necessary in order to deal with this pain. I'll address this issue further in the next section.

When disengagement from immersion occurs because of criticism, the artist's reaction can vary. One musician told me that through years of composing and performing, she had developed a thick skin. In fact, she believed that anyone who hoped to survive as an artist must learn not to take criticism personally. But she also reported avoiding reading reviews of her work, and she avoided looking at Internet discussions about her performances because she still felt vulnerable to negative feedback. "I don't think I could deflect too much negative critique, so I've learned not to look at all."

An artist's underlying confidence in his artistic talent determines a large part of his resilience in the face of criticism. So, also, does his experience of safety within artistic immersion: if artistic immersion is usually a gratifying experience and he is usually viewed favorably by his audience, he will be able to withstand and bounce back from an occasional hit without a huge disruption to his process.

Two cinematic examples nicely illustrate different artist responses to critique. Although these excerpts are artistic portrayals of Mozart and Jackson Pollack, interpreted through both screenwriters and actors, they struck me and have stayed in my mind as poignant illustrations of different reactions to criticism. The first is a scene from the movie *Amadeus*, in which Mozart presents his latest opera for the royal court. The king responds, "It was, it was ... something wrong that I can't put a finger on ... It has too many notes. Yes, that's what it is; the ear can only handle a certain number of notes. It has too many notes."

"Too many notes?" Mozart exclaims. "And what notes would you recommend that I remove? No, it has the perfect number of notes, not too many and not too few. It has exactly the number of notes that it requires."

The film portrays Mozart as an obnoxious, immature young man who challenged his elders and societal norms, an irresponsible prankster who had a loud and annoying laugh and rebelled with sexual and alcoholic binges. He was serious only when it came to his music. Confident to the point of arrogance, Mozart was convinced that his music was "better than all others" and made no compromises in his composition or performance. He shrugged off negative feedback easily, believing his opinion was correct and all others were without value.

At the other end of the spectrum is the portrayal of Jackson Pollock in the movie *Pollock*, which shows the painter as alcoholic, socially inept, and insecure. He is quite sensitive to the feedback from others about his paintings. The viewer gets the impression that he is initially tentative in his confidence as an artist. He seems brittle, as if the slightest criticism of his work might send him into an alcoholic binge or even suicide. He does not seem to have anything else in his life — no relationships, no money, no spirituality. All he has is his painting, and even that feels fragile.

His first art show is well received. A couple of notable art critics are impressed with his work and appreciate its originality and uniqueness. His sense of specialness is bolstered. However, a little later in the film, one critic says that one of his paintings has "too much blue in it." "I don't like the blue," the critic says. Pollock is visibly injured and defensive. "You think it misses? What should I do to fix it? I'll fix it.

You want the color more quiet? You think it should be a different color of blue?" Pollack starts to paint over what he had already done, when this same critic then says, "It's your art — you're not going to destroy your art, are you? No, this painting is something." Pollack puts down the paint and settles back into himself.

Pollock had such a fragile self-esteem that he had little confidence in his own perceptions. He needed the approval of others about his work to sustain his emotional stability. The film portrays an interesting parallel in his life: when his new genre of painting was being applauded by critics and the public, he was also able to establish a loving and intimate relationship with a woman for the first time in his life. For a while he stopped drinking, and it seemed that the relationship strengthened his capacity to paint, and his painting strengthened his capacity for intimacy.

However, when his popularity rose and reporters and critics began to intrude on his immersive state (being filmed at work for a documentary, for example), he was thrown into disengagement from his art. He had little resilience, little ability to bounce back from disruptions to his process. In a state of tortured disengagement, he turned away from his art and from his relationship with his lover.

When he lost immersive connection with his painting, he had nowhere to go for reconsolidation. Instead, he turned to alcohol for an immersive experience. But rather than feeling enhanced and strengthened by the drinking, he found the alcohol only served to numb his pain of isolation. All of his hurts, disappointments, and aloneness didn't heal. They were buried behind the alcohol and eventually led him to total despair and suicide. This tragic story illustrates the importance of empathic others in the process of creativity.

Availability of Understanding/Empathic Others

The greatest barrier to the process of creativity is aloneness. By aloneness I do not mean merely the absence of others. I mean aloneness in one's inner world — the secret world where we experience these breaks or fractures in our sense of self. When we cannot share this level of our experience with others — our hopes and fantasies alongside our injuries, doubts, fears, and insecurities — we are vulnerable to a disruption in our creative process or even in the continuity of our mental health in general.

The means by which a person understands the internal world of another is through empathy. Having empathy is putting oneself in the other's shoes, trying to imagine what the other person is experiencing on the inside. It is an effort to understand — not to fix, reassure, or even agree with the other person. It is an attempt to find the sense and the reasonableness in the other person's feelings, beliefs, and perceptions. "I can see why you would feel that way" and "It makes sense that you would think that" are typically experienced as empathic statements. Paradoxically, receiving empathy from another person will usually melt whatever negative experience we are having or at least moderate its intensity so it is less of an obstacle in our process.

The power of empathy to comfort, soothe, strengthen, and revitalize is almost magical. Any experience is more bearable if someone is with us. The most frightening, painful, and empty feelings arise when we are alone in the world. Especially when we are feeling depleted or broken, the sense of aloneness can multiply our fear and doubt.

I am amazed at how many people exist in a shell of inner aloneness. Empathy is the hallmark of any effective psychotherapy; no matter what theoretical approach a therapist uses, therapy will be ineffective if the patient does not feel that the therapist understands him. It is sad how many people experience my empathy in therapy as something new. "I've never had someone be so curious about my feelings and reactions," or "It is so nice that you get it, what it's like for me, and that you seem to believe that it makes sense . . . that I make sense."

Many people have experienced such a lack of empathy from others that they have given up on communicating about their inner life. "They would think I'm crazy" and "I'm not supposed to feel this way" are fears that inhibit expression. Could it be that many artists have tended to experience their art as the safest way to express their inner life — when interpersonal intimacy has been untrustworthy or unavailable? If this is the case, then reaching out for empathic connections with others may be a threatening experience in itself. When in a state of disengagement, particularly one that involves a deterioration of confidence or stability, the artist may not have the reserve of courage to risk further exposure to others. And, indeed, we all need to carefully distinguish who is a trustworthy recipient of our inner lives. To reveal our innermost hurts and fears to someone who is unlikely to understand and who may respond to our vulnerability without empathy would be self-destructive. No, we must be careful and deliberate about whom we can trust with the most sensitive parts of ourselves.

If loved ones, or those people closest to us, do not seem to have the capacity for an empathic appreciation of our inner life, a peer group may be the safest bet for an understanding response. Being able to share our ups and downs with others who are traveling a similar path will help us to feel less alone. These peers are likely to be understanding because they have been there and need the same thing. There is strength and comfort with like-kind, especially during periods of disengagement.

There are many ways to find peer groups, including actual meetings as well as online communities. Writers' groups can be found through bookstores, universities, online postings, conferences, and other avenues. Attend a creative writing class or sign up for a writing workshop or retreat. Visual artists can find twinship experiences in studios, galleries, art associations, and conferences, as well as through art classes and workshops. Musicians can connect through various performance venues, online forums, classes, and concerts.

Availability of Other Immersive Realms

The immersive experience itself is strengthening and generates hope. Artistic immersion has been our focus, but recall that immersion can be experienced in many different realms. When artistic immersion breaks apart into disengagement, the artist can restore his energy and courage by turning to other immersive experiences.

Intimate love and friendship relationships can be felt as immersive and can supply the as-one experience. Emotional, physical, or sexual intimacy can reconsolidate a beleaguered sense of self and can regenerate creativity, hope, and strength.

Immersing into a child's world can also be helpful. If you don't have children of your own, it can be vitalizing to spend time with nieces, nephews, or children of friends who trust you. Experiencing a child's enthusiasm, openness, and capacity to play can recharge us. Play with them, enter into their world, suspend your rationality. When we can find empathy for their experience and enter into their internal lives, we are more apt to discover immersive connections with them. Being able to be a trustworthy provider of empathy to a child can also increase our own sense of adequacy.

Many artists discover that appreciating the art of others can be restorative and inspiring. In a state of disengagement from their own artistic expression, they can immerse into the art of another to generate their own creativity and hope. Other works of art can feed the artist's soul and can provide immersive experience if the viewer opens himself to the experience.

Spirituality can also be an immersive encounter. Being able to experience faith and beauty in a higher power of some sort can regenerate creativity and hope, which are often obscured during disengagement.

Psychotherapy can also be an available type of alternative immersive experience. As I have already described, in addition to increasing cognitive understandings of what's going on, therapy can be an immersive encounter in its own right and can help the artist through various phases of the creative process.

Other potential realms of immersive experience include sports, hobbies, academic study, and all types of new learning. Rather than being distractions from the creative process, these other involvements may actually help the artist to sustain and restore his creative capacity.

All in all, sustaining the creative process involves a continuous movement in and out of immersive states and realms. When disengagement occurs in one realm, immersion into a different realm can restore and strengthen the artist so he can reenter — and so on and so on.

Understanding Your Underlying State of Self

There is considerable debate in psychoanalytic dialogue about the nature of the state of the self at any given point. In one corner are the theoreticians who believe that a person's psychological constitution is developed and determined during early childhood. They believe that the nature of a child's experiences early in life sets her character strengths and weaknesses. The resulting personality is relatively firmly fixed and static. The child will carry these fundamental tendencies and vulnerabilities throughout life and will tend to approach all life experiences from this position. So, for example, a child who was abused will always have difficulty trusting and feeling safe with others. This understanding describes the continuity of our experience over time and the feeling that we are the same person despite changes in our circumstances, relationships, and age.

In the other corner are those theoreticians who believe that a person's self state is determined entirely by the current context of relationships. Who I am at any given moment is determined by who I am with and by the unique and changing dynamics within a particular relationship. In this view, self-perception is fluid and changing, created anew with different relationships and at different points in time. This view understands how a person can feel confident in one relationship or context and insecure in another and clearly rejects the notion of a fixed personality or identity.

My position lies between the two. I believe that early life does, indeed, help to develop a person's basic personality. Childhood experiences with others form basic prototypes of what it is like to be with others. The fundamental assumptions about what to expect from others and what one has to offer to others are developed in our earliest relationships with parents and other caregivers. In this way, we carry ourselves with us into all of our later experiences. We carry certain tendencies and vulnerabilities and certain areas of confidence and strength. But I do not view the self as static and isolated. Our current experiences and relationships can challenge and change our underlying assumptions and fears. There is a hope for a new beginning in every relationship, and there is renewed hope for a reconstruction of our old self and old fears in every experience.

With all this being said, the artist brings a certain set of fundamental fears and coping responses to every artistic endeavor. The artist who has had, by and large, good enough reflections of her specialness, the availability of strong and supportive figures, and a solid sense of fitting in and belonging with others will be psychologically equipped to handle the bumps and bruises in the creative journey. This is not to say that she will not experience fear, self-doubts, or insecurities. But an artist with this kind of solid psychological base will be able to bounce back readily and will be able to reach out for the kinds of support that she needs from others to help her along the way.

The artist who has not enjoyed a steady supply of psychological support from others may experience the ups and downs of the creative process more painfully. These current injuries may reopen deep wounds from his past that are more difficult to heal. This artist may not trust that others will supply what he needs. He may have needed to detach so completely from his own feelings and needs because they were not previously recognized or responded to that he does not even know what to ask for. This artist, then, is likely to try to handle periods of disengagement by himself.

It is when a person is isolated (alone with this internal world) that he is most vulnerable to symptoms such as depression and anxiety. In addition, when he does not have available others or an alternative immersive realm to turn to, he is at risk of turning to drugs, alcohol, or other behaviors to seek comfort. The person can get wrapped up in this alternative, feel encased by it and lost in it. But rather than generating strength and hope, it works by deadening not just the pain but all feeling. It supplies a temporary fix to the longing for immersion and a Band-Aid for the pain of the injury. And it serves as a temporary companion to soothe his sense of aloneness. But it is ultimately empty and leaves the person feeling more lost and helpless than before.

Psychotherapy may be necessary in order to help this person out of the downward spiral. By creating another possibility for immersive experience, hopefully this person can experience another realm of connection that can strengthen and revitalize him.

Acceptance: Let It Be

Experienced and successful artists come to recognize and accept their own individual tendencies and patterns in the dance of immersion. We all hope that entry into immersion will become increasingly safer with each gratifying experience. But even many prolific artists continue to struggle with, and be tortured by, the fears associated with immersion.

The natural human reaction to feeling pressured is to resist. When we pressure ourselves to be in a different place, we are placing another layer of resistance on top of already existing fears. Expecting or commanding ourselves to immerse will likely backfire.

Recognizing and accepting our natural tendencies when it comes to immersing with our artwork and with other people can help us accept times of disengagement. It seems that genetics may play a part in determining our comfort zones in connection and disengagement. Studies of parent-infant interactions by Beatrice Beebe, Daniel Stern, Frank Lachman, and others have demonstrated that babies are born with varying levels of the need for connection. Some babies reach out for nearly constant connection with their parent, and others are more comfortable with degrees of distance. Baby and parent are involved in a constant, largely unconscious relational dance of engagement and disengagement. In one study, Beebe and Stern videotaped the interactions of mother-baby pairs and then watched the videotapes frame-by-frame. In this microsecond analysis, it was evident that some babies sought more eye contact and physical contact with their mothers than other babies. In fact, in some pairs, the infant rejected attempts by the mother to connect by looking away from her, in effect taking alone time in the only way possible for an infant. Relational problems often developed if the baby and mother did not match each other's natural tendencies in the interpersonal dance of connection and disengagement.

There is the same dance in our relationship with artwork. Disengagement from creative immersion is a natural part of the process. Sometimes we need more distance, sometimes less. But if we learn to respect and honor the need to disengage, without attaching negative meanings to it, we can use it as a time to relax, regenerate, and consolidate ourselves.

Through my experience working with artists, I have realized there is a broad spectrum of natural individual differences in their flow between immersion and disengagement. From one author who writes every day, to a painter who paints only on the weekends, to a composer who works only in spurts, with long gaps in between — much of their discomfort about being in a space of disengagement has been lessened by an awareness of their own individual patterns and by accepting their need for disengagement as part of the process.

THE FINAL DISENGAGEMENT

Still, there is a calm, pure harmony, and music inside of me.

— VINCENT VAN GOGH

A picture lives by companionship. It dies by the same token. It is therefore risky to send it out into the world. How often it must be impaired by the eyes of the unfeeling.

— MARK ROTHKO

After an artist has invested his entire self in a project, moving in and out of immersive connection with it perhaps hundreds of times, there comes a point when he knows it is finished. How does an artist know when his work is complete? It is most often an internal sense of simply knowing. It is the moment when the painter goes to brush another stroke but stops, having nothing more to paint. One more stroke would be too much, would be redundant, or would begin to deconstruct the form already present.

Matisse said, "[I know] when it expresses my emotion as completely as possible. It is at that point when the sense of resonance is enduring and durable. The artist, while assessing the work, does not experience anxiety, depression or fragmentation, but sureness and calm. The artist no longer feels compelled to change the work because it feels balanced and complete. The work is done. It exists as a thing in itself."

Internally, the artist has the experience of full expression. "I've said what I have to say," he feels, "and I've expressed it in the best way that I can." There is an immediate feeling of satisfaction, a decompression of the intense investment, only moments before, of psychological and emotional energy. He experiences a calmness that is only felt after a thorough and pure expression of the soul. And because the artwork originated from the heart of the artist's being, and creating it involved his total immersion into its expression, the finished product is experienced as perfect expression.

In all spheres of life, whether artistic, interpersonal, or spiritual, hope is generated from this immersive experience of fully expressing ourselves. When we can feel this, we feel gratified. It is the risking in this self-expression that is the hard part. But once we find the courage to engage these meaningful parts of ourselves, we feel gratification and contentment.

At the moment of artistic completion, audience response is not considered. The gratification of perfect expression or perfect engagement, which is reflected in the artwork, is the artist's barometer of success. Only later may the artist become concerned about audience response. But for the moment, the experience of fulfillment through the finished artwork is enough.

Following this experience of gratification, the artist begins to disengage from the work. Because it is finished and already holds all relevant meaning, she no longer feels it as an immersive connection. The previously experienced immersion with the project is no longer needed. This final disengagement from the artwork is what allows artists to sell their work to others and to move on to their next creation. Its purpose now is to communicate with others, to be understood and appreciated, and the artist lets go of it toward this end.

I once heard a saying that seemed initially paradoxical: "Good relationships are easier to leave than bad ones." At first, this made no sense to me, but I have come to appreciate its truth in many realms of life. In a good relationship, the person is strengthened in the connection, making it easier to feel confident to go on without the relationship. This person has been supported and has experienced immersion with another as a safe and trustworthy experience. If this relationship ends, the person is left with the hope, and indeed the assumption, that he or she will be able to re-create a positive connection.

But in bad relationships, both individuals are torn down and diminished in the process. Relationships marked by blame and distrust deteriorate each person's strength and trust in self and others. These people look toward the future with fear and dread that they will repeat these negative experiences. Thus, it can be harder to feel the confidence to leave such relationships, as the fear of aloneness and lack of future connection can be paralyzing.

Likewise, if the artist has had a difficult relationship with his artwork, disengagement from it will be more painful or may even be avoided. This artist may feel diminished by the creative experience. He may hold on to the work, never really feeling that he is finished or that it is an adequate reflection of his intentions. He may avoid beginning another project out of the fear of repeated frustration and pain.

However, when an artist has had a good enough relationship with his project, it is often easier for him to disengage from it when it is completed. He has gained strength and hope in the immersive experience with the art, and he is free to move on to his next project with increased trust in his capacity for immersion. He comes out of the process a little more integrated, a little more hopeful, and a little more solid. He trusts the creative process a little more so that immersing in the next project is a little less frightening.

As the painter Mark Rothko put it: "Pictures must be miraculous: the instant one is completed, the intimacy between the creation and the creator is ended. He is an outsider. The picture must be for him, as for anyone experiencing it later, a revelation, an unexpected and unprecedented resolution of an eternally familiar need."

Creating a work of art requires perseverance and persistence. When we truly appreciate the psychological challenges involved in the process of immersion-disengagement-reentry, works of art become even more amazing and magical. Understanding how many times you must stand at water's edge and take a dive into the unknown helps us all to appreciate artists and their work even more. Let us return to where we began, with C. S. Lewis's *Pilgrim's Regress*:

> "Come on, John," said Vertue, "the longer we look at it the less we shall like it." And with that he took a header into the pool and they saw him no more. And how John managed it or what he felt I did not know, but he also rubbed his hands, shut his eyes, despaired, and let himself go. It was not a good dive, but, at least, he reached the water head first.

GUIDES

I. UNDERSTAND THE TYPE OF DISENGAGEMENT YOU ARE EXPE-
RIENCING.

Were you interrupted by external demands or realities? Tend to these needs and activities so you can reengage with a clear head. Are you recovering from an intense immersive connection? Get sleep, exercise, eat, laugh, and play. Are you disengaged because you hit a glitch or a stumbling block in your work? Take time to step back from it. Engage with other people, immerse in other activities. Often, resolutions and insights will present themselves when you are not directly thinking about the problem. Did the artistic content become emotionally threatening or overwhelming? Again, take your needed emotional distance from the artwork so you can integrate and assimilate what emotions or experience you confronted. Reach out for emotional support from empathic others. See a therapist. Then take some time to find your new center after feeling connected with someone and understood. Are you waiting for feedback about your work-in-progress? Find twins who can appreciate your feelings of tension and vulnerability. Start another project: try to distract yourself with other immersive activities. Are you feeling overexposed? Reach out for connections with supportive others and try to feel the strength in vulnerability. Are you feeling deflated or diminished because your work has been criticized or rejected? Find empathy for yourself. Of course, you are feeling deflated. Reach out for mirrors who will reflect your strengths; know that your heroes have coped with similar rejections and have continued with success; connect with twins who can appreciate your pain and offer you comfort.

2. STOP PRESSURING YOURSELF TO REENGAGE.

Try to relax and understand the reason for your disengagement. If you can make sense of what is blocking you, you have taken the first step in getting past the block. Understanding is more important than fixing — once you understand what you are dealing with, then you can become creative in your problem-solving efforts or even in allowing yourself to "be where you're at." Reach out for supportive others. And know that the more you try to force yourself to move ahead too quickly, the more you are likely to resist. Respect the fears you are facing and respect the difficulty in facing these challenges.

Incomplete Sentence Prompts

The following incomplete sentence prompts are designed to help you become aware of and clarify your internal assumptions, fears, and fantasies. It is usually best to complete each sentence without lingering: fill in the sentence with the first thought that comes to mind. You can write longer responses in your journal. Feel free to write as much or as little as you like. You will begin to see patterns in your responses that can help you to examine your hopes, fantasies, fears, and assumptions at a deep and meaningful level.

FANTASIES

1. I have always fantasized about being a _____.
2. If I could win an award, it would be for _____.
3. I always used to play, as a child, that I was _____.
4. I'd never tell anyone, but my wish is to _____.
5. If I had the courage, I would _____.
6. Sometimes I dream that I am _____.
7. Sometimes I daydream about being _____.

SELF-PERCEPTION

1. If I could improve one thing about me, it would be _____.
2. I believe I am basically _____.

3. My greatest strength is _____.
4. My greatest weakness is _____.
5. When I get scared, I _____.
6. When I fail at something, I _____.
7. I feel best when I am _____.
8. The best compliment I ever got was _____.
9. I am good at _____ but not at _____.

FEARS

1. My most humiliating experience was when I _____.
2. I get most anxious before I _____.
3. The one thing I could never do would be to _____.
4. My scariest dream was _____.
5. My biggest fear is _____.
6. The part of me that I keep most hidden is _____.
7. Most people believe that I am _____.
8. The worst criticism a person could make of me would be to say that I am _____.
9. If I really let down my defenses, I believe I would _____.
10. My biggest secret is _____.
11. If I have a nightmare, it is usually about _____.
12. I get most frightened when other people _____.
13. I am most worried about a loved one when _____.
14. When I'm with other people, I am afraid they are thinking that I _____.

SUPPORT STRUCTURES

1. The best thing my mother gave me was _____.
2. The best thing my father gave me was _____.

3. The most important thing my mother failed to give me was _____
_____.

4. The most important thing my father failed to give me was _____
_____.

5. My mother was proud of me for _____.
6. My father was proud of me for _____.
7. My mother was ashamed that I _____.
8. My father was ashamed that I _____.
9. My mother was afraid that I would _____.
10. My father was afraid that I would _____.
11. The person who understood me best as a child was _____.
12. My brother/sister viewed me as _____.
13. _____ could always count on me for help.
14. My family really appreciated my ability to _____.
15. If I had a nickname, it was _____.
16. Those people closest to me don't realize that I need _____
_____.

17. I would never ask someone to _____ for me.
18. People would usually _____ when I showed them my work.
19. My parents tried to control my _____.
20. I always controlled my _____.
21. I could always count on _____ for help.
22. I never needed any help when I was _____.
23. Asking for help _____.
24. It is hard for me to receive _____ from others.
25. It is hard for me to give _____ to others.
26. I could really relax when I was with _____.

193

Acknowledgments

The emphasis I've given in this book to the central importance of others in the creative process makes this section especially meaningful. I truly could not have completed this book, nor the subsequent and sometimes emotionally brutal process of trying to get it published, without the mirrors, heroes, and twins that grace my life. Writing this book has given me a reason to reach out to and connect with others when I might not have otherwise. To those I owe my sincerest thanks and appreciation for taking the time and love to help me along and for, often, being a mirror with me at one moment, a hero with me at another, and a twin with me at still another.

I have, indeed, lived this book as I have written it, experiencing every facet of my fears and my dreams: the thrill of recognition and acknowledgment alternating with the plummeting of self-confidence and fear of demolishment. Mike, my husband and colleague, has ridden the ride and has been present with me, as well as contributing theoretical, conceptual, and editorial ideas. Our discussions about the ideas in the book and how they relate to our own experiences have helped me to clarify and expand my thinking. In actuality, this book is as much Mike's as it is mine, and its completion is a reflection of how creativity is born out of the experience of connectedness.

I started to write this book when my son was eleven. Now Alex is sixteen, a young man whose growth has paralleled the book's creation.

I cannot express how deeply enhancing the experience of parenting has been, and how Alex's and my relationship has propelled me to keep reaching, keep developing, and keep learning right alongside him. I think I've gotten equal strength both from my being a hero to Alex and from Alex being a hero to me.

And I also thank Liana, my now-grown stepdaughter, for her help and encouragement and for being a model of intellectual energy and determination.

The first book I ever wrote was called *English Is Our Own*. I wrote this grammar textbook for fourth-graders when I was a fourth-grader. In support of my writing, my mom and dad helped me to make a book cover from cardboard, fabric, and homemade glue. I have remembered ever since then that Dad posed a challenge to me at the time: to see which of us could get a book published first. Well, Dad has had many things published since that time, but our bet has remained alive in my mind over the years and has always felt like a foundation of my parents' support and belief in me. Throughout the process of writing and selling this book, Mom and Dad have been constant sources of strength, inspiration, and comfort, as well as contributing editorial help.

My brother, Joe, has also supported and helped me every little step of the way. Being an author himself, he was a constant source of information, empathy, and twinship. My sister, Judy, has also been an enthusiastic presence to me, and our shared loves of Peter Gabriel and chimps has propelled me along in the writing and has also given us some tremendous laughs.

Jason Gardner, my editor, has been absolutely wonderful. His appreciation of these ideas has given me considerable self-confidence, vitality, and energy for writing. I could not have wished for a more collaborative, enjoyable, and gratifying engagement. His respect for the creative process is apparent, and his input reflects his fluid capacity to understand both me and the reader. I feel very lucky that I and this book found a home with Jason and New World Library. Everyone at New World has made me feel like part of the family, which has meant more to me than I can say.

Meredith Bernstein, my agent, believed in this project and supported and encouraged me through the process of finding a publisher. I deeply appreciate her wisdom and patience and feel she has mentored me into the publishing world in a kind and empathic way. Meredith, you and I are a good fit even if you didn't go to Ohio University!

I owe much of my clinical knowledge and skill as a therapist to my mentor and friend Anna Ornstein, MD, and her husband, Paul Ornstein, MD. Anna facilitated a study group of psychologists for fifteen years, and it was within this collaboration that I learned the real art of psychotherapy and blossomed as a professional. Study group became like a family for us, Anna being our "good mother" for whose attention, affirmation, and acknowledgment we all good-naturedly competed. Her keen and reasonable way of understanding people helped us all to develop special relationships with our patients and with each other.

Speaking of my siblings in study group, this book is for and from all of us, as we have energetically discussed these ideas during countless happy hours and dinners. Although many people have moved through study group over the years, our core group has consisted of Medford Moreland, PsyD, Todd Walker, PsyD, John Tidd, PsyD, Stan Dudley, PhD, and me.

My deepest gratitude goes to the many artists I have worked with over the years. Each has expanded my appreciation and respect for the creative process, and I am touched by the trust they have shown me in revealing their innermost hopes and fears. These relationships have certainly been mutually enhancing, because although I was identified as the helper in my role of therapist, each of them has also helped me along in my process of writing this book.

A special thank-you goes to Loren Long, who believed in this project enough, even before I had an agent or a publisher, to take time from his painting to talk with me. I also want to especially thank Karen Moning, a good friend who encouraged me to write this book in the first place and who is living proof that dreams actually can come true.

So many friends and colleagues have supported me and this project in many different ways: Doris Brothers, PhD, Karen Schwartz, PhD, Deidre Knight, Susan Berg, Barbara Hummel, LPC, Curt Spear, PhD, Kathy Smithson, Bettina Hohls, Peter Rocjewicz, PhD, Awadagin Pratt, Carol Press, PhD, George Hagman, PhD, Lenny and Al Katz, Amy Prater, Betty Malo, Karen and Bob Miday, both MDs, Fred Gensler, MD, Tracie Bonet, Robyn Horst, Janet Zack, and all the bright and creative folks who meet in cyberspace on the PG Full Moon Club.

A special acknowledgment goes to Peter Gabriel, who has inspired, energized, and comforted me for most of my life through his music. Although he doesn't know it, his music has helped me immerse in dance, in writing, and in love.

Notes

Chapter One: The Challenge of Immersion

20 *Rollo May, a psychologist who has written extensively about creativity* R. May, *The Courage to Create* (New York: Bantam, 1975), quote at p. 39.

21 *A picture is not thought out and settled beforehand* Picasso, quoted in E. Protter, *Painters on Painting* (Mineola, NY: Dover Publications, 1997), p. 202.

21 *Carl Rotenberg referred to this immersive experience* C. Rotenberg, "Self-Object Theory and the Artistic Process," in *Learning from Kohut: Progress in Self Psychology*, vol. 4, ed. A. Goldberg (Hillsdale, NJ: The Analytic Press, 1988), see pp. 193–213.

22 *The image offered us by reading the poem* G. Bachelard, *The Poetics of Space* (Boston: Beacon Press, 1964), p. xix.

24 *Karen Walant explores how addictions can serve* K. Walant, *Creating the Capacity for Attachment: Treating Addictions and the Alienated Self* (Northvale, NJ: Jason Aronson, 1995).

28 *A man's mind, once stretched by a new idea* O. W. Holmes, Sr. *The Autocrat of the Breakfast Table* (Boston: The Atlantic Monthly, 1858).

30 *On the floor I am more at ease* Jackson Pollock, quoted in Protter, *Painters on Painting*, p. 253.

31 *Creative people tend to alternate* H. Kohut, *Self Psychology and the Humanities* (New York: Norton, 1985), p. 114.

36 *I said to my soul, be still* T. S. Eliot, "East Coker," *The Complete Poems and Plays* (New York: Harcourt, Brace and Company, 1952), p. 127.

Chapter Two: The Light and Dark of Immersion

39 *Destruction of the world that we have built* Although in his text, Campbell is referring to mythological images in dreams, I find this a suitable description for creativity as well.

45 *I would like to be rich enough* Degas, quoted in Protter, *Painters on Painting* (Mineola, NY: Dover Publications, 1997), p. 127.

49 *Sure, sometimes I go through periods of real despair* Willem de Kooning, quoted in Protter, *Painters on Painting*, p. 242.

Chapter Three: The Need for Others

70 *D. W. Winnicott (1886–1971), a British psychoanalyst, proposed* D. W. Winnicott, *Playing and Reality* (New York: Basic Books, 1971), pp. 119, 5; emphasis in original.

70 *the psychoanalyst Michael Balint emphasized the importance of seeking out and enjoying "symbiotic experiences"* M. Balint, *The Basic Fault: Therapeutic Aspects of Regression* (New York: Brunner/Mazel, 1979), p. 65.

72 *Daniel Stern, a prominent researcher in child development* D. Stern, *The Interpersonal World of the Infant: A View from Psychoanalysis and Developmental Psychology* (New York: Basic Books, 1984), p. 105.

74 *mankind's natural orientation is to be immersed in relationships* K. Walant, *Creating the Capacity for Attachment: Treating Addictions and the Alienated Self* (Northvale, NJ: Jason Aronson, 1995), p. 60.

77 *I want to touch people with my art* In *Vincent van Gogh: A Self-Portrait in Arts and Letters*, ed. H. Anna Suh (New York: Black Dog & Leventhal Publishers, 2006), p. 44, letter to Theo van Gogh, April 1882.

Chapter Four: Finding Strength in Mirrors

79 *looked at and admired* H. Kohut, *The Restoration of the Self* (Madison, CT: International Universities Press, 1977), p. 137.

84 *Though Virginia Woolf's work was well respected* L. DeSalvo, "Tinder-and-Flint: Virginia Woolf and Vita Sackville-West," in *Significant Others: Creativity and Intimate Partnership*, ed. W. Chadwick and I. Courtivron (London: Thames and Hudson, 1993), p. 86.

86 *I have always sought to be understood* H. Matisse, quoted in J. Elderfield, *Henri Matisse: A Retrospective* (New York: Museum of Modern Art, 1992), p. 168.

Chapter Five: Finding Inspiration in Heroes

95 *Heinz Kohut, the father of contemporary psychology theory* H. Kohut, "Discussion of 'The Unconscious Fantasy' by David Beres," in *The Search for the Self*, vol. 1, ed. P. H. Ornstein (New York: International Universities Press, 1978; paper orig. pub. 1961), pp. 309–18; quote at p. 310.

95 *The idealized other is one who is "gazed at in awe"* H. Kohut, *The Restoration of the Self* (Madison, CT: International Universities Press, 1977), p. 437.

96 *A dream described in Rollo May's book* R. May, *Man's Search for Himself* (New York: Dell Publishing, 1953), p. 86.

Notes

97   *In 1875 Auguste Rodin traveled to Florence* F. V. Grunfeld, *Rodin: A Biography* (New York: Henry Holt, 1987), p. 95. Rodin's involvement with Claudel is described on pp. 159–212.

98   *Anthony Storr describes how artistic talent is often apparent in childhood* A. Storr, *The Dynamics of Creation* (New York: Ballantine Books, 1972), p. 41.

100 *the Juilliard School in New York* M. Chermayeff, "Juilliard," on *American Masters*, PBS, January 2003.

104 *Franz Kafka is believed to have attributed almost magical powers* See M. Brod, *Franz Kafka: A Biography* (London: Secker & Warburg, 1948).

107 *D. W. Winnicott wrote extensively about compliance* D. W. Winnicott, *The Maturational Processes and the Facilitating Environment* (New York: International Universities Press, 1965), p. 44; emphasis in original.

Chapter Six: Finding Comfort in Twins

112 *the interaction of a baby monkey with its contemporaries* H. F. Harlow, "The Primate Socialization Motives," in *Social Psychiatry*, vol. 1, ed. Ari Kiev (London: Routledge & Kegan Paul, 1970), p. 402.

114 *I imagined many books born out of our intimacy* A. Nin, "Alraune," published as "Djuna" in *The Winter of Artifice* (Paris: Obelisk, 1939); reprinted as "Hans and Johanna," *Anaïs: An International Journal* 7 (1989): 3-22.

114 *soulmates, fleshmates, unique contributors* P. Jason, "Dropping the Other Veil," *Anaïs: An International Journal* 6 (1988): 32.

Chapter Seven: Connecting with the Audience and Meeting Deadlines

124 *New research on parent-infant interaction* See D. Stern, N. Bruschweiler-Stern, and A. Freeland, *The Birth of a Mother: How the Motherhood Experience Changes You Forever* (New York: Basic Books, 1998); and B. Beebe and F. Lachman, *Infant Research and Adult Treatment: Co-constructing Interactions* (Hillsdale, NJ: The Analytic Press, 2002).

Chapter Eight: Approaching Immersion

140 *Darwin's revolutionary idea of natural selection* A. Storr, *The Dynamics of Creation* (New York: Ballantine Books, 1972), pp. 60–61.

146 *Very gradually I have discovered ways of writing* B. Russell, "How I Write," in *Portraits from Memory and Other Essays* (London: Allen & Unwin, 1965), p. 195.

Chapter Nine: Diving In

156 *The painting rises from the brushstrokes* Joan Miró, quoted in R. Fitzhenry, *The Harper Book of Quotations*, 3rd ed. (New York: HarperCollins Publishers, 1993), p. 52.

156   *As your carving progresses* R. A. Baillie, quoted in D. Gotshalk, *Art and the Social Order* (New York: Dover Publications, 1962), p. 74.

158   *The songs made me, not I them*; and *an occult Power was moving the pen* Goethe and Thackeray, respectively, both quoted in R. E. M. Harding, *An Anatomy of Inspiration*, 2nd ed. (Cambridge: Heffer, 1942), pp. 14–15.

159   *I cannot really say the book was written* Thomas Wolfe, quoted in B. Ghiselin, *The Creative Process* (Berkeley: University of California Press, 1952), p. 195.

160   *Every line has been produced by me with labor-pangs* S. T. Coleridge, quoted in A. Chandler, *Beauty and Human Nature: Elements of Psychological Aesthetics* (New York and London: Appleton-Century Co., 1934), p. 338.

160   *I dread writing poetry* S. Spender, "The Making of a Poem," in *Critiques and Essays in Criticism*, ed. R. W. Stallman (New York: Ronald, 1949), p. 28.

161   *A picture used to be a sum of additions* Picasso, quoted in E. Protter, *Painters on Painting* (Mineola, NY: Dover Publications, 1997), p. 202–3.

161   *Every child is an artist* Picasso, quoted in Fitzhenry, *Harper Book of Quotations*, p. 50.

162   *It is in playing and only in playing* D. W. Winnicott, *Playing and Reality* (New York: Basic Books, 1971), p. 64.

Chapter Ten: Coping with Disengagement and Reentry

166   *Coleridge described how he wrote "Xanadu"* S. T. Coleridge, "Xanadu: The Ballad of Kubla Khan," in *Christabel*, 2nd ed. (London: William Bulmer, 1816).

176   From the film *Amadeus*, screenplay by Peter Shaffer, directed by Milos Forman (Saul Zaentz Company, 1984).

177   From the film *Pollock*, screenplay by Barbara Turner and Susan Emshwiller, based on the book by Steven Naifeh and Gregory White Smith, directed by Ed Harris (Sony Pictures Classics, 2000).

185   *videotaped the interactions of mother-baby pairs* B. Beebe and D. Stern, "Engagement-Disengagement and Early Object Experiences," in *Communicative Structures and Psychic Structures*, ed. N. Freedman and S. Grand (New York: Plenum, 1977), pp. 35–55.

186   *[I know] when it expresses my emotion* Matisse, quoted in A. Barr, *Matisse: His Art and His Public* (New York: The Museum of Modern Art, 1951), p. 286.

188   *Pictures must be miraculous* Mark Rothko, quoted in E. Protter, *Painters on Painting* (Mineola, NY: Dover Publications, 1997), p. 239.

189   *"Come on, John," said Vertue* C. S. Lewis, *The Pilgrim's Regress* (William B. Eerdmans Publishing, 2002; orig. pub. 1933), p. 168.

Bibliography

Atwood, G. E., and R. Stolorow. *Structures of Subjectivity*. Hillsdale, NJ: The Analytic Press, 1984.

Bachelard, G. *The Poetics of Space*. Boston: Beacon Press, 1964.

Balint, M. *The Basic Fault: Therapeutic Aspects of Regression*. New York: Brunner/Mazel, 1968.

Barr, A. *Matisse: His Art and His Public*. New York: The Museum of Modern Art, 1951.

Beebe, B., and F. Lachman. *Infant Research and Adult Treatment: Co-constructing Interactions*. Hillsdale, NJ: The Analytic Press, 2002.

Beebe, B., and D. Stern. "Engagement-Disengagement and Early Object Experiences." In *Communicative Structures and Psychic Structures*, ed. N. Freedman and S. Grand. New York: Plenum, 1977.

Bollas, C. *Forces of Destiny: Psychoanalysis and Human Idiom*. London: Free Association Books, 1989.

————. *The Shadow of the Object: Psychoanalysis of the Unthought Unknown*. New York: Columbia University Press, 1987.

Bowlby, J. *Attachment*. New York: Basic Books, 1969.

————. *Loss: Sadness and Depression*. New York: Basic Books, 1980.

————. *Separation: Anxiety and Anger*. New York: Basic Books, 1973.

Brod, M. *Franz Kafka: A Biography*. London: Secker & Warburg, 1948.

Campbell, J. *The Hero with a Thousand Faces*. New York: Princeton University Press, 1949.

Chandler, A. *Beauty and Human Nature: Elements of Psychological Aesthetics*. New York and London: Appleton-Century Co., 1934.

Cook, J., ed. *The Book of Positive Quotations*. Minneapolis: Fairview Press, 1993.

Csikszentmihalyi, M. *Flow: The Psychology of Optimal Experience*. New York: Harper Perennial, 1990.

DeSalvo, L. "Tinder-and-Flint: Virginia Woolf and Vita Sackville-West," in

Significant Others: Creativity and Intimate Partnership, ed. W. Chadwick and I. Courtivron. London: Thames and Hudson, 1993.

Fitzhenry, R., ed. *The Harper Book of Quotations*. New York: HarperCollins Publishers, 2005.

Gallo, A., and P. Gabriel. *Peter Gabriel*. Rome: One Love Production, 1986.

Ghiselin, B. *The Creative Process*. Berkeley: University of California Press, 1952.

Gotshalk, D. *Art and the Social Order*. New York: Dover Publications, 1962.

Grunfeld, F. V. *Rodin: A Biography*. New York: Henry Holt, 1987.

Hagman, G. "The Creative Process." In *Progress in Self Psychology*, vol. 16, ed. A. Goldberg. Hillsdale, NJ: The Analytic Press, 2000.

Harding, R. E. M. *An Anatomy of Inspiration*, 2nd ed. Cambridge: Heffer, 1942.

Harlow, H. F. "The Primate Socialization Motives." In *Social Psychiatry*, vol. 1., ed. Ari Kiev. London: Routledge & Kegan Paul, 1970.

Jung, C. *Man and His Symbols*. New York: Doubleday, 1964.

Kligerman, C. "Art and the Self of the Artist." In *Advances in Self Psychology*, ed. A. Goldberg. New York: New York University Press, 1980.

Kohut, H. *The Analysis of the Self*. Madison, CT: International Universities Press, 1971.

———. "Discussion of 'The Unconscious Fantasy' by David Beres." In *The Search for the Self*, vol. 1, ed. P. H. Ornstein. New York: International Universities Press, 1978; paper orig. pub. 1961.

———. *How Does Analysis Cure?* Chicago: University of Chicago Press, 1984.

———. "Introspection, Empathy, and Psychoanalysis: An Examination of the Relationship between Mode of Observation and Theory." In *The Search for the Self*, vol. 1, ed. P. H. Ornstein. New York: International Universities Press, 1978.

———. *The Restoration of the Self*. Madison, CT: International Universities Press, 1977.

———. *Self Psychology and the Humanities*. New York: Norton, 1985.

Lemkow, A. F. *The Wholeness Principle: Dynamics of Unity within Science, Religion, and Society*. Wheaton, IL: Theosophical Publishing House, 1990.

Maisel, E. *Coaching the Artist Within: Advice for Writers, Actors, Visual Artists and Musicians from America's Foremost Creativity Coach*. Novato, CA: New World Library, 2005.

———. *Creativity for Life: Practical Advice on the Artist's Personality and Career from America's Foremost Creativity Coach*. Novato, CA: New World Library, 2007.

May, R. *The Courage to Create*. New York: Bantam, 1975.

———. *Man's Search for Himself*. New York: Dell Publishing, 1953.

Meltzoff, A. "Foundations for Developing a Concept of Self: The Role of Imitation in Relating Self to Other and the Value of Social Mirroring, Social Modeling, and Self Practice in Infancy." In *The Self in Transition: Infancy to Childhood*, ed. D. Cicchetti and M. Beeghly. Chicago: Chicago University Press, 1990.

————. "The Roots of Social and Cognitive Development: Models of Man's Original Nature." In *Social Perception in Infants*, ed. T. Field and N. Fox. Norwood, NJ: Ablex, 1985.

Miller, J. P. *Using Self Psychology in Child Psychotherapy: The Restoration of the Child*. Northvale, NJ: Aronson, 1996.

Mitchell, S. *Hope and Dread in Psychoanalysis*. New York: Basic Books, 1993.

Mondrian, P. "Plastic Art and Pure Plastic Art." In *Art and Its Significance: An Anthology of Aesthetic Theory*, ed. S. D. Ross. Albany, NY: SUNY Press, 1937.

Opie, I., and P. Opie. *The Classic Fairy Tales*. New York: Oxford University Press, 1974.

Ornstein, A. "The Dread to Repeat and the Hope for a New Beginning: A Contribution to the Psychoanalysis of the Narcissistic Personality." In *The Annual of Psychoanalysis*, vol. 2. New York: International Universities Press, 1974.

————. "The Dread to Repeat: Comments on the Working-Through Process in Psychoanalysis." *Journal of the American Psychoanalytic Association* 39 (1991): 377–98.

————. "Self Pathology in Childhood: Developmental and Clinical Considerations." *Psychiatric Clinics of North America* 4, no. 3 (1981): 435–53.

————. "Supportive Psychotherapy: A Contemporary View." *Clinical Social Work* 13 (1986): 14–30.

Protter, E. *Painters on Painting*. Mineola, NY: Dover Publications, 1997.

Rotenberg, C. "Selfobject Theory and the Artistic Process." In *Learning from Kohut: Progress in Self Psychology*, vol. 4, ed. A. Goldberg. Hillsdale, NJ: The Analytic Press, 1988.

Sander, L. "The Regulation of Exchange in the Infant-Caretaker System and Some Aspects of the Context-Context Relationship." In *Interaction, Conversation, and the Development of Language*, ed. M. Lewis and L. Rosenblum. New York: Wiley, 1977.

————. "Toward a Logic of Organization in Psycho-Biological Development." In *Biologic Response Styles: Clinical Implications*, ed. K. Klar and L. Siever. Washington, DC: Monograph Series, American Psychiatric Press, 1985.

Stern, D. *The Interpersonal World of the Infant: A View from Psychoanalysis and Developmental Psychology*. New York: Basic Books, 1984.

————. *The Motherhood Constellation*. New York: Basic Books, 1994.

————. *The Present Moment in Psychotherapy and Everyday Life*. New York: W. W. Norton, 2004.

Stern, D., N. Bruschweiler-Stern, and A. Freeland. *The Birth of a Mother: How the Motherhood Experience Changes You Forever*. New York: Basic Books, 1998.

Stolnitz, J. *Aesthetics and Philosophy of Art Criticism: A Critical Introduction*. Boston: Houghton Mifflin Company, 1960.

Stolorow, R. "Critical Reflections on the Theory of Self Psychology: An Inside View." *Psychoanalytic Inquiry* 6 (1986): 387–402.

Stolorow, R. D., and G. E. Atwood. *Contexts of Being: The Intersubjective Foundations of Psychological Life*. Hillsdale, NJ: The Analytic Press, 1992.

Storr, A. *The Dynamics of Creation*. New York: Ballantine Books, 1972.

Tolpin, M. "Strivings of the Healthy Self: The Psychoanalysis of Normal Development — Selfobject Transferences." Paper presented at the Toronto Child Psychotherapy Conference, Toronto, Canada. November 14, 1996.

Walant, K. *Creating the Capacity for Attachment: Treating Addictions and the Alienated Self*. Northvale, NJ: Jason Aronson, 1995.

Wang, W. *The Emergence of Language Development and Evolution*. New York: W. H. Freeman and Company, 1989.

Williamson, M. *A Return to Love: Reflections on the Principles of "A Course in Miracles."* New York: HarperCollins, 1992.

Winnicott, D. W. *The Maturational Process and the Facilitating Environment*. New York: International Universities Press, 1965.

———. *Playing and Reality*. New York: Basic Books, 1971.

Wolf, E. *Treating the Self: Elements of Clinical Self Psychology*. New York: Guilford Press, 1988.

Woolf, V. *The Diary of Virginia Woolf*. Edited by Anne Oliver Bell. New York: Harcourt Brace Jovanovich, 1978.

Index

A

acceptance, 184–85
acting, criticism of, 90
Adaptation (film), 137
addiction, 2, 24, 53–55
alcohol, 24, 53–55, 56, 178, 184
Alcoholics Anonymous, 55
aloneness, 178–80
alter egos. *See* twins/twinship
Amadeus (film), 176–77
anger, 52–53, 107–8
annihilation, fear of, 33
anxiety, 24, 51, 85, 174
art appreciation, 21–22, 151, 181
art/artwork
    artist's relationship with, 8
    audience-driven, 20–21
    completion of, 186–88
    immersion of self into, 160–62
art associations, 180
artist
    narcissistic/self-centered stereotype, 86
    tortured/isolated stereotype, 76–77,
      104–5
arts, visual
    darkness and, 56–59
    immersion in, 20, 21, 30–31, 59
    visualizations vs. finished products, 90
audience
    art driven by, 20–21
    artistic completion and, 187
    artist's relationship with, 59
    assumptions about, 122–29, 133–34
    blocking out, 123–24
    blocks caused by, 41–42
    childhood relational history and, 124–26

connection with, 121–22, 129–31
creative process and, 9–10, 121–22
fantasies about, 122–23, 143–44, 153
Guides, 133–34
imagining connection with, 75–77, 84–85
immersion sought by, 130–31
rebellion and, 107–8
autonomy, Western culture's emphasis on, 68,
    132
avoidance, 145–46, 148

B

Bachelard, Gaston, 22
Baillie, R. A., 156–57
Balint, Michael, 70–71
Basic Fault, The (Balint), 70–71
Beebe, Beatrice, 185
Beethoven, Ludwig van, 141
Blake, William, 159–60
blocks
    author's experience, 46–47
    case studies, 3–4, 40–45
    childhood history and, 84–85
    to connection with heroes, 102–8
    as fears of connection, 7–8
    Guides, 60–62
    to immersion, 32–33, 40–44, 50–51
    psychological problems resulting from,
      2, 9, 141
    to specialness, 86–93
    understanding/respecting, 11, 25–26,
      40, 60–61
    See also fears
boundaries, 132
Bowlby, J., 65
Brahms, Johannes, 141

Index

About the Author

Anne Paris, PhD, is a clinical psychologist in private practice in Cincinnati, Ohio, who specializes in helping artists and other creative people reach their potential. She founded the Cincinnati Center for Self Psychology, a training and education center for mental-health professionals. She is an adjunct professor in the Union Institutes graduate psychology program where she teaches classes, supervises and trains graduate psychology students, and participates in doctoral committees. Dr. Paris has practiced psychotherapy for over twenty years, specializing in creativity, trauma, relationships, and parenting. She was trained and mentored in Self Psychology and Intersubjectivity Theory by the internationally known experts Anna Ornstein, MD, and Paul Ornstein, MD. Dr. Paris lives in a house in the woods with her husband, Mike, her son, Alex, and two cats, Katie and Morgan. Her website is www.anneparis.com.